Hebrews

THE NEARNESS OF KING JESUS

LISA HARPER

LifeWay Press®

Nashville, Tennessee

LOVINGLY DEDICATED to the B3 sisterhood:
Rachel Beavers, Christy Dismukes, Judy Flaherty,
Paige Greene, Paige Hill, Katie Holliday, Melanie
Jeansonne, Carissa Pereira, B. K. Steib, and
Heather Whittaker. There is no other group of
girls I'd rather vault over comfort zones and
charge up mountains with—B3s forever, baby!

Also dedicated to Kelley Beaman, an honorary
B3 who refused to tote a backpack for fifty
miles but prayed for us every step of the way,
fed us when we returned from the battle of
the blisters, and graciously opened up her
lake house to film some of this Hebrews
study, including our watery leap of faith!

Published by LifeWay Press®

© 2013 Lisa Harper

ISBN 978-1-4300-2559-7

Item 005592096

Dewey decimal classification: 227.87

Subject headings: BIBLE. N.T. HEBREWS—STUDY \ WOMEN \ GOD

To order additional copies of this resource, write to LifeWay Church Resources Customer Service; One LifeWay Plaza; Nashville, TN 37234-0113; fax 615.251.5933; phone 800.458.2772; email orderentry@lifeway.com; order online at www.lifeway.com; or visit the LifeWay Christian Store serving you.

Printed in the United States of America

Adult Ministry Publishing

LifeWay Church Resources

One LifeWay Plaza

Nashville, TN 37234-0152

CONTENTS

"A BIBLE THAT IS FALLING APART USUALLY BELONGS TO SOMEONE WHO ISN'T."

–CHARLES SPURGEON

ABOUT THE AUTHOR

Rarely are the terms "hilarious storyteller" and "theological scholar" used in the same sentence, much less used to describe the same person, but Lisa Harper is anything but stereotypical. She is a master storyteller, whose writing and speaking overflows with colorful pop culture references that connect the dots between the Bible and modern life.

Her vocational resume includes six years as the director of Focus on the Family's national women's ministry, followed by six years as the women's ministry director at a large church. Her academic resume includes a master's in theological studies with honors from Covenant Seminary. Now a sought-after Bible teacher and speaker, Lisa is currently featured on the national Women of Faith tour and speaks at many other large multi-denominational events—such as Kathy Trocoli's Among Friends, LifeWay's women's events, and Women of Joy conferences—as well as at hundreds of churches all over the world. She's been on numerous syndicated radio and television programs and was featured on the cover of *Today's Christian Woman*.

She's written 11 books, including *Overextended … and Loving It!*, *Stumbling into Grace,* and *A Perfect Mess*. In spite of her credentials, the most noticeable thing about Lisa Harper is her authenticity. "I'm so grateful for the opportunities God's given me," Lisa says, "but don't forget: He often uses donkeys and rocks!"

INTRODUCTION & GROUP SUGGESTIONS

Mindy, one of my friends at The Next Door (a six-month residential addiction recovery program where I volunteer) plopped down on a couch beside me with an exaggerated sigh and said, "This stuff is *hard*, Lisa."

I gave Mindy's shoulders a squeeze and asked, "What's hard, Sweetie?"

She leaned back as far as the couch would allow and replied, "EVERY. THING. Everything here is hard." Then she launched into her daily routine at TND:

> Wake up at 5:00 a.m. to get ready for work.
> Walk to the bus stop—regardless of the weather—to catch the 6:15 cross-town bus.
> Ride bus to Krystal, then fry burgers/deal with irate customers/clean toilets for 8 hours.
> Catch the bus back to The Next Door.
> Eat a quick dinner.
> Help clean up the kitchen.
> Attend a mandatory community meeting and/or devotional.
> Attend a mandatory AA meeting.
> Take a shower and go to bed, while showing grace to a noisy roommate.
> Start all over again the following morning.

With a partial smile on her face and tears in her eyes, she lamented, "I'm not used to working this hard, Lisa. I mean, good night, I just got here from prison a few weeks ago, and all I had to do there was lay around and watch cable. I promise, I'm trying as hard as I can and I don't wanna get kicked out of the program, but it's dang hard to go from not working at all for six years to busting my tail overnight!"

I couldn't help but think of Mindy's bumpy transition when I flipped through this Hebrews workbook. I couldn't help think about the precious it's-been-a-while-since-I've-been-in-church or the I've-never-been-in-a-small-group-and-didn't-know-crop-pants-were-required girls who will also flip through these pages and then probably break out in a cold sweat. Because it's all new to them and, at first glance, being in a Bible study sounds like hard work! Especially if they aren't familiar with Scripture and they're afraid one of us with a dog-eared Bible and a Vera Bradley tote full of highlighters will turn up our nose or, worse still, feel led to expose her inexperience.

So let's agree to make Hebrews an easy place to engage with God. A place where every woman feels like it's OK to ask questions about Him, share the highs and lows of her story, and ultimately lean further into the nearness of King Jesus. Therefore, it's not necessary to choose a single leader for this study (I can almost hear the audible gasps from the type A's reading this!), and may be more beneficial to choose a couple of friendly chicks to co-lead, which will help the environment be less personality-driven and more participation-driven.

A FEW TIPS TO PROMOTE HEALTHY INVOLVEMENT:

- Establish a no-monopoly chat zone. Encourage everyone to answer at least one question rather than having one big-talker answer all of them.

- Allow for "silence cushions" between questions to give introverts time to formulate their thoughts and participate.

- Throw spitballs at anyone who responds to a question with a basic yes-or-no answer. OK, maybe spitballs are a tad punitive, but encourage real responses!

- Be quick to listen and slow to give advice or attempt to fix the other chicks' problems in your circle. Just say no to Dr. Phil wannabes!

- Make your best effort to begin and end on time.

- Don't focus on moving through all the material each time you get together; instead, focus on how your small-group tribe is moving toward Jesus.

To make Hebrews user-friendly, we've created a workbook/journal geared toward participation instead of intimidation. We've also segmented the workbook into chunks instead of days, so you can complete the questions when you have time—when your baby's sleeping, when your husband's glued to a football game, or when you're finally home from work and have changed into a pair of comfy sweatpants. The last thing we want is to make the homework so difficult and time-consuming that your group dwindles down to nonexistent.

Each week starts with a two-page video and group guide. For the first session, you'll just watch the video and get to know each other. Then, during the following week, complete your first week's study. When you gather for the second week, discuss the week 1 study and watch the second week's video.

Your format can depend on your group's size. If your group has few members, discuss the previous week's study first and then watch the video, allowing for some time to discuss the video's questions afterward. If you have a large group, watch the video first and then combine the discussion of video questions and the previous week's work.

Now, may I encourage you to breathe deeply, smile genuinely (even if it's just to yourself), and turn the page? Then doodle wildly in the margins. Be as honest as possible in every response. And fire away with your thoughts, since few questions have right or wrong answers. Feel free to throw this workbook on the floor with gusto if something I've written steps on one of your emotional bruises ... or hug it close to your chest when Jesus whispers how valuable you are to Him while you're perusing a passage.

My deep hope and fervent prayer is that the King of all kings will woo us closer to Himself than ever this season. That God's Spirit—our Comforter and Counselor—will cause us to long for a more intimate relationship with our Redeemer and compel us to share more compassion with the poor, lost, and marginalized world around us. I want to love bigger, fear less, and run headlong into the arms of Jesus every single day as a result of hiking through Hebrews with you. I really can't wait to see how God shows up in this adventure!

Warmest regards,

Lisa

As an extra feature of Hebrews, we have included six articles excerpted from *Biblical Illustrator* magazine. Feel free to ignore the articles or to do the extra study. For the complete version of the articles and nine additional articles on Hebrews, you may purchase the downloadable set from *Biblical Illustrator*. Look for "Hebrews: The Nearness of King Jesus Biblical Illustrator Bundle" on *lifeway.com/hebrews*. *Biblical Illustrator* is a great enrichment magazine for Bible teachers and students. It delves into archeology and biblical history with photos and insights that help bring Scripture to life.

OPTIONAL BONUS

You will find two bonus videos in the Hebrews leader kit: a panel discussion of the difficult issues in the Book of Hebrews and a guest teaching segment with Mandisa on Hebrews 12:1-2. You might choose to have an extra session to view and discuss these segments or you could use them for a celebration to end the study.

If you're on social media, please share what you're learning at #nearJesus

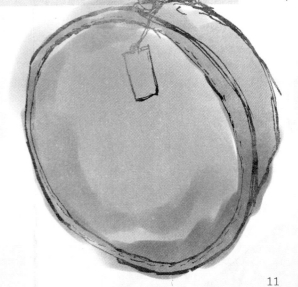

The Book of Hebrews covers two key Christological concepts: the _____ and the _____ of Jesus.

Hebrews was written sometime between A.D. _____ and _____ , approximately three to four decades after the death and resurrection of Jesus.

Hebrews was written to a small group of _____ Christians, who were living in either _____ or _____ .

Monotheistic: pledging one's allegiance to _____ God

Polytheistic: pledging one's allegiance to a plethora of little "g" gods

Nero confused the _____ .

> Long ago, at many times and in many ways, God spoke to our fathers by the prophets, but in these last days he has spoken to us by his Son, whom he appointed the heir of all things, through whom also he created the world. He is the radiance of the glory of God and the exact imprint of his nature, and he upholds the universe by the word of his power. After making purification for sins, he sat down at the right hand of the Majesty on high, having become as much superior to angels as the name he has inherited is more excellent than theirs.
> HEBREWS 1:1-4 (ESV)

_____

_____

_____

_____

_____

_____

Video sessions available for purchase
at www.lifeway.com/hebrews

What are four of the "many ways" (polytropos) God used to speak to His people long ago?

1. _____

2. _____ *and* _____

3. _____

4. _____ *and* _____

The "latter days" or "last days" refers to the time period on the continuum of progressive revelation between the _____ and _____ coming of Christ.

Discussion Questions:

1. *How has Hebrews ministered to you in the past?*

2. *What has been your steepest climb in the past? How has Jesus helped you to keep on?*

3. *What climb do you face now? What would you like to get from this group and study?*

_____

_____

_____

_____

_____

_____

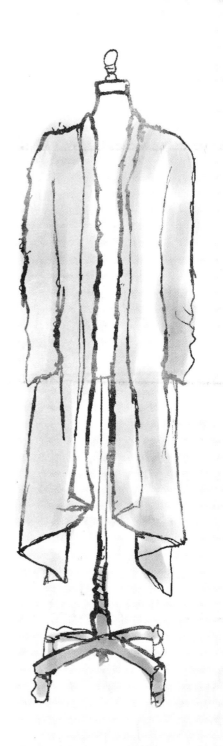

ANGELS ROCK BUT JESUS RULES

WALK A MILE IN HEBREW SHOES

I rarely feel like I'm about to burst with excitement when I'm on a plane. At Starbucks, yes. Pottery Barn, yes. Anywhere that serves tableside guacamole and free chip refills, most definitely. But in a motorized aluminum tube? Probably not. Since I travel about two hundred days a year, my mindset on planes is more eye-rolling resignation than wide-eyed enthusiasm. The seats are configured to a supermodel's bottom. And I often end up in a middle seat, squashed between two NFL linemen-sized guys with questionable hygiene. To add insult to injury, they inevitably hog the armrests. Needless to say, the travel part of my job can be a tad unpleasant, as well as claustrophobic.

On this particular transatlantic flight, however, I didn't mind being crammed or even having Cran-Apple juice accidentally sloshed in my lap. I was going to Hillsong Church in London— the top entry on my church bucket list. I've been singing along with their worship CDs since the '90s and have listened to scads of Hillsong sermons online, so to visit one of their main campuses was a dream come true for me. Plus, I was traveling with my dear friend, Christine Caine, who's one of my favorite chicks in the universe and just happens to be part of Hillsong's international teaching team. It was like being en route to the chocolate factory with Willy Wonka himself!

We spent four whirlwind days in London, watching God do amazing things. Hundreds of people put their hope in Jesus, the worship music was so anointed that I wept the whole time we were singing, plus I got mocha lattes between all four services, making the whole experience even more heavenly.

The only less-than-wonderful moment in London happened at a dinner the Hillsong pastors had arranged with some new members at their gorgeous home in a very chic neighborhood. Christine mentioned there would be several interesting people at the dinner—a runway model, an incredibly successful venture capitalist, and some other European bigwigs—so I knew to dress up, but I'd run out of appropriate things to wear. It snowed the whole time we were there, and I hadn't packed accordingly. So, with about an hour to get ready, I decided to race to a few stores and buy a new outfit.

I had completely forgotten how much smaller UK sizing is from our generously pro-portioned American clothes. After forty-five minutes of berating myself for too much chips-and-guacamole consumption (because I couldn't find pants that would fit over my thighs or a jacket that didn't give me sausage arms), I had only fifteen minutes to buy something, jog back to the hotel, change, reapply makeup, and fluff my hair. At that very moment, I passed the Anthropologie store window and noticed a pretty peach mohair sweater on the mannequin. *That'll go perfectly with my dark jeans and the long strand of pearls I packed,* I thought. So I barreled into the store, bought the sweater without trying it on, and hustled back to the hotel.

As soon as I glanced at the full-length mirror in my room, I knew I was in trouble. I resembled a horror-movie-sized fuzzy lollipop—not unlike the Michelin Man in the first *Ghostbusters* movie. What in the world compelled me to think a bright orange-yellow, hairy sweater would look good stretched across my not-exactly-petite top half? Of course, by then I had about 90 seconds to meet our group in the lobby, so I had no choice but to spritz perfume on my furry, sorbet-colored self, square my shoulders, and walk downstairs with my head held high.

The situation escalated into an even greater opportunity in humility when our driver dropped us at our dinner engagement. Our host, who met us at the door, was exactly eye-level with my bottom rib, since I had worn really high heels that night in an attempt to elongate and slenderize my appearance. In reality, I just made myself unnaturally tall. My pastel largeness may have alarmed the wee host, because his greeting was brief. Then he swung the front door wide open to his mansion.

That is when I noticed EVERY. SINGLE. PERSON. In the room was dressed from head to toe in black. And not fuddy-duddy, funereal black either—they were clad in butter-soft black leather ensembles, flowing black silk dresses, and effortlessly elegant black tailored jackets. Furthermore, EVERY. SINGLE. PERSON. Looked like they ate approximately four carrot sticks and one vitamin-that-makes-your-hair-shiny per day.

To their credit, those lean Londoners did not gasp out loud when I—a woolly, brightly hued American—lumbered into their sophisticated midst. A few eyes might've initially widened in surprise; however, after just a second's hesitation, they all moved forward and enveloped me like incredibly gracious swans making a protective circle around a fashion-challenged duckling.

I won't trouble you with further details about my total-opposite-of-a-Cinderella evening, except to say that after making lots of small talk and nibbling on foie gras (what in the world is wrong with pigs in a blanket as an appetizer?), I had humiliation further etched into my soul while walking across a glass ceiling during a tour of the lovely home. The architect thought a solid glass ceiling smack dab in the middle of six other floors would be an interesting feature, our host explained. While everyone else marveled over the architect's brilliance, I secretly plotted to toilet paper his home, because he obviously didn't factor in non-waifish Yanks in high heels who would be forced to take mincing steps across his crystal-clear masterpiece, terrified of crashing through said ceiling and accidentally squishing a former Vogue model. After which, the Yank would be indicted on accidental homicide charges and never, ever get to return to her homeland where people wear brightly colorful outfits and the average woman's size is twelve (two points better than a perfect ten, if you ask me).

The next time you're at a dinner party with church friends, casually throw out the phrase "ontological equality," which basically means that the three members of the Trinity—God the Father, Jesus the Son, and the Holy Spirit—are equal in value but different in their function.[1] It'll make you sound smart, and, more important, it'll help you remember the doctrinal concrete the writer of Hebrews used for his church members' theological foundation.

THE LORD'S SONG IN A STRANGE LAND

In Psalm 137:4 the singer asked, "How shall we sing the LORD's song in a foreign land?" I sure didn't feel like singing at that London party, but I suspect we've all felt out of place at one time or another. So now it's your turn. I'd love to hear your story as well. If I could be there with you, we could laugh together or at least commiserate.

When was the last time you were aware of not fitting in at a social, work, or church setting?

What do you think it was/is about you that didn't gel with those surroundings?

What kind of emotion did your sticking-out-like-a-sore-thumb experience stir up in your heart?

My awkward London debut reminded me of what it feels like to be a square peg in a round hole. Or a donkey at the Kentucky Derby. My feelings, however, probably only represent a tiny taste of the unease our Jewish Christian friends felt in the second half of the first century, because they completely clashed with their culture too. Remember, Hebrews believed in one true God, while their Roman neighbors believed in a smorgasbord of false gods (they even adopted the gods of people they defeated in battle, just to cover all their bases).

HEBREW PRACTICE	ROMAN PRACTICE
Try to live holy, righteous lives.	If it feels good, do it.
Choose marriage and family.	Have multiple partners and abandon female infants on the side of the road.

Although I doubt they had to tiptoe across glass ceilings, these Jewish Christians did have to walk through each day not knowing if they were going to make it home for dinner. Not knowing if one of the emperor's Christian-hating cohorts would snatch them off the street and set them on fire for sport—which is a million times worse than being the only peach bobbing in a sea of cool black.

When has your faith in Jesus caused you to feel awkward or not fit in?

When you don't fit in because of your faith, how do you feel?

What's the worst persecution you've faced from being a Christian?

Have you ever felt physically threatened or unsafe because of your belief in Jesus? If so, describe that situation.

Talk with your group about how we, who have mostly been safe, can identify with and support those who are physically persecuted for their faith in other parts of the world.

LEAN INTO THE STORY

Before we dig into the rich soil of this text, I want to remind you that the Hebrews were living in uber-scary times. Their businesses were being ransacked, their kids were being bullied, and some of their Christian friends had been martyred for their faith. I doubt many of us have experienced the level of persecution they did in their everyday lives, but I bet most of us can identify with being at least a little afraid.

STOP AND THINK ABOUT IT FOR A MINUTE.

Have you ever been climbing up or down a steep staircase and felt like you were going to fall? ❏ *yes* ❏ *no*

Have you ever been a passenger in another person's speeding car and felt like you were going to crash? ❏ *yes* ❏ *no*

Have you ever ridden a roller coaster at an amusement park and felt like you were going to become one with the earth below? ❏ *yes* ❏ *no*

If you said yes to any of those situations, how did you react? You grabbed the banister or the handle above the car window or the metal crossbar—which, along with gravity, was the only thing keeping you in that stupid roller coaster, right? When we're frightened, it's human nature to reach for something solid, something that will anchor us to safety, something that will keep us from tumbling into Scary Town.

Jesus is the only thing we can hang on to that will actually support us in tough times. So the pastor (that is, the writer) of Hebrews keeps reminding his anxious parishioners about Jesus' better-than-anything-else nature.

In this second part of his sermon, the pastor of the Hebrews makes the case for the Son's supremacy to angels. Hebrews 1:5-14 is a treasure chest of theological booty, but we'll examine just two of the brightest jewels. The first is the author's use of multiple quotations from the Old Testament to contrast Jesus and angels.

We've set aside the entire next page to show some of the quotations and allusions the pastor uses in verses 5-14. But before you examine them, consider the following details about how the New Testament writers used Scripture.

How the New Testament Writers Use the Old Testament

You will note as you study Hebrews that almost everything the pastor said was either a direct quote of the Old Testament or an allusion to it. However, you may struggle with the wording for several reasons.

First, the people of Bible times had no experience with our modern idea of exact quotations. Remember, they lived in an world of oral learners. They spoke the Word. They learned it by hearing it. Books were far too rare for people to have their own copies. They lived and breathed the Scripture to such a degree that we sometimes cannot determine exactly which Old Testament passage was being referenced. The writer/speaker might weave multiple passages together.

Second, note that the Greek Septuagint was the Bible most in use in the first century. It was a translation of the Hebrew manuscripts. Any translation results in some degree of paraphrasing because human languages never match perfectly. We live in an unbelievably blessed time because thousands of scholars have spent their entire working lives comparing manuscripts and seeking the most accurate original documents of Scripture. Therefore we have multiple excellent translations to compare and study.

Finally, we must recognize that the writers of the New Testament wrote under unique inspiration of the Holy Spirit. For example, in Hebrews 10:20 the pastor said Jesus opened a new and living way to God's presence. The pastor said Jesus' crucified body was the torn veil in the temple. God inspired the writer of Hebrews to make such a claim, but today, we cannot produce new ideas that equal God-breathed Scripture. We seek to understand the completed message God has given us, not to add novel teachings to it.

Hebrews 1:5 cites Psalm 2:7: "I will tell of the decree: The LORD said to me, 'You are my Son; today I have begotten you.'" And 2 Samuel 7:14: "I will be to him a father, and he shall be to me a son. When he commits iniquity, I will discipline him with the rod of men, with the stripes of the sons of men."

Hebrews 1:6 cites Deuteronomy 32:43: "Rejoice with him, O heavens; bow down to him, all gods, for he avenges the blood of his children and takes vengeance on his adversaries. He repays those who hate him and cleanses his people's land."

Hebrews 1:7 cites Psalm 104:4: "He makes his messengers winds, his ministers a flaming fire."

Hebrews 1:8 cites Psalm 45:6-7: "Your throne, O God, is forever and ever. The scepter of your kingdom is a scepter of uprightness; you have loved righteousness and hated wickedness. Therefore God, your God, has anointed you with the oil of gladness beyond your companions."

Hebrews 1:9 cites Isaiah 61:1,3: "The Spirit of the Lord GOD is upon me, because the LORD has anointed me to bring good news to the poor; he has sent me to bind up the brokenhearted, to proclaim liberty to the captives, and the opening of the prison to those who are bound."

Hebrews 1:10 cites Psalm 102:25-27: "Of old you laid the foundation of the earth, and the heavens are the work of your hands. They will perish, but you will remain; they will all wear out like a garment. You will change them like a robe, and they will pass away, but you are the same, and your years have no end."

Hebrews 1:13 cites Psalm 110:1: "The LORD says to my Lord: 'Sit at my right hand, until I make your enemies your footstool.'"

In Hebrew, the Book of Psalms is titled Tehillim, which means "songs of praise."[2] And since each psalm was originally crafted as a song, that makes Psalms the first collective hymnal of the Israelites—kind of like God's iPod!

When David began Psalm 110 with "The LORD says," he established the lyrics that follow as an oracle—a direct statement from God. It's also clear that David intended this song to be messianic in nature because of the way he describes God as speaking to his future king: "The LORD says to *my Lord*" (emphasis mine).[3]

Keep in mind that these believers were practicing Jews before they put their hope in Jesus. It's safe to say they were very familiar with the Old Testament—it was their Bible. Most of them had been listening to *Tanakh* (the Jewish Bible) readings and singing psalms since before they relinquished their pacifiers. So their pastor connects the dots and proves God's new revelation by citing the old revelation, illuminating the fact that Jesus is the fulfillment of the Old Testament prophecies. The pastor's many allusions to Scripture also underscore the truth that we can always mine jewels from our past, even if the only beauty they provide is the reminder of what God has rescued us from.

Which of those messianic "song lyrics" (Psalm 2:7; 45:6-7; 102:25-27; 104:4; and 110:1) would you be most prone to sing?

Why do those particular words resonate with you?

The Jewish Bible is also known as the Tanakh. Tanakh is not a word but an acronym, T-N-K, based on the three divisions of the Hebrew Bible—Torah (the Law), Nevi'im (the Prophets), and Ketuvim (the Writings).[4]

In royal courts, a king extended his scepter toward subjects when he wanted them to approach his throne—when he wanted them to come closer (Psalm 45:6-7). How have you experienced King Jesus beckoning you nearer to His throne recently?

The second jewel we're going to examine is the way the pastor proclaims the superiority of Jesus over angels:

Jesus is God's Son; therefore His name is superior to angels: "[H]aving become as much superior to angels as the name he has inherited is more excellent than theirs. For to which of the angels did God ever say, 'You are my Son, today I have begotten you'? Or again, 'I will be to him a father, and he shall be to me a son'?" (Hebrews 1:4-5)

Jesus is God's Son; therefore His position is superior to angels: "And, again, when he brings the firstborn into the world, he says, 'Let all God's angels worship him.'" (Hebrews 1:6)

Angels worship Jesus; therefore His nature is superior to theirs: "Of the angels he says, 'He makes his angels winds, and his ministers a flame of fire.'" (Hebrews 1:7)

Jesus' reign is forever; therefore His role is superior to angels: "But of the Son he says, 'Your throne, O God, is forever and ever, the scepter of uprightness is the scepter of your kingdom.'" (Hebrews 1:8)

Jesus created the world; therefore His work is superior to angels: "'You, Lord, laid the foundation of the earth in the beginning, and the heavens are the work of your hands; they will perish, but you remain; they will all wear out like a garment, like a robe you will roll them up, like a garment they will be changed. But you are the same, and your years will have no end.'" (Hebrews 1:10-12)

Jesus sits at God's right hand; therefore His destiny is superior to angels/ministering spirits: "And to which of the angels has he ever said, 'Sit at my right hand until I make your enemies a footstool for your feet'? Are they not all ministering spirits sent out to serve for the sake of those who are to inherit salvation?" (Hebrews 1:13-14)

At this point, you might be tempted to feel sorry for angels because it does seem like the pastor-author is being a bit harsh. I mean, good night, it's OK to casually note Christ's superiority, but this kind of diatribe could send Gabriel and his fellow angels to counseling for a few millennia. So let me digress and review something we recently discussed.

Remember the Roman smorgasbord of gods and fake faiths? It included the heresy of dualism, which essentially proposed that the physical world—everything we can touch, taste, see, or feel—was unholy, while the spiritual or intangible world had greater value. Sleazy dualism salesmen argued that angels were therefore higher on the "divine ladder" that led to God because they didn't inhabit human bodies or rub shoulders with "filthy" people like lepers and prostitutes and tax collectors.

Unfortunately, some of the Jewish converts had bought into this hogwash-peddled-as-higher-learning, probably because angels had always been important in Jewish history. For example, when Moses gave the Israelites his last blessing, he lauded the angels who'd accompanied Yahweh during the miracle on Mt. Sinai:

> The Lord came from Mount Sinai
> and rose like the sun from Edom;
> he showed his greatness from Mount Paran.
> He came with thousands of angels
> from the southern mountains.

DEUTERONOMY 33:2 (NCV)

So it's no wonder the Hebrews got all Abbott-and-Costello-ish, becoming confused about Who was on first and needing to be set straight.

Good teachers will flat straighten out a student if she misunderstands an important concept. For goodness' sake, if they didn't, can you imagine how many goggle-wearing ninth graders would accidentally set their desks on fire during chemistry class? How much more important it was for the spiritual teachers of the early believer—the one on whose shoulders the New Testament church was built—to rectify any Christological confusion.

In describing angels as wind and fire (Hebrews 1:7), the author is emphasizing that God created angels to execute His will. What adjectives or metaphors would you use to describe angels?

Read the following passages about angels (all in HCSB). Mark the responsibilities that describe what an angel does.

1 Kings 19:5: "Then he lay down and slept under the broom tree. Suddenly, an angel touched him. The angel told him, 'Get up and eat.'"

Isaiah 6:6-7: "Then one of the seraphim flew to me, and in his hand was a glowing coal that he had taken from the altar with tongs. He touched my mouth with it and said: 'Now that this has touched your lips, your wickedness is removed and your sin is atoned for.'"

Ezekiel 9:1: "Then He called to me directly with a loud voice, 'Come near, executioners of the city, each of you with a destructive weapon in his hand.'"

Daniel 8:18-19: "While he was speaking to me, I fell into a deep sleep, with my face to the ground. Then he touched me, made me stand up, and said, 'I am here to tell you what will happen at the conclusion of the time of wrath, because it refers to the appointed time of the end.'"

Matthew 18:10: "'See that you don't look down on one of these little ones, because I tell you that in heaven their angels continually view the face of My Father in heaven.'"

Mark 13:27: "'He will send out the angels and gather His elect from the four winds, from the end of the earth to the end of the sky.'"

Acts 7:53: "'You received the law under the direction of angels and yet have not kept it.'"

Galatians 3:19: "Why then was the law given? It was added because of transgressions until the Seed to whom the promise was made would come. The law was put into effect through angels by means of a mediator."

In light of these verses, what responsibilities would you include as part of an angel's job description?

Did any of these tasks come as a surprise to you? If so, which one(s)?

Why do you think modern-day Christians are often hesitant to engage in conversations about angels?

SCOOT YOUR CHAIR A LITTLE CLOSER TO JESUS

One of my favorite movies of all times is *To Kill A Mockingbird* (based on Harper Lee's classic novel, published in 1960). The storyline is based on a tough-on-the-outside-tender-on-the-inside attorney by the name of Atticus Finch (played by Gregory Peck). Atticus is limping gruffly through life—with his two young children skipping carefully behind him—in the aftermath of his wife's untimely death. But then he makes a life-changing choice that ultimately galvanizes his fractured little family. He decides to become the defense attorney for an innocent black man named Tom, who's been framed for raping a white girl in their small, Southern, segregated town.

My favorite scene in the film takes place soon after Tom is convicted, even though everyone in the courtroom knows he's not guilty—especially after the excellent, impassioned defense Atticus has presented. Nonetheless, the all-white jury chooses tradition over truth and unfairly hands down a guilty verdict. Prejudiced rednecks whoop with glee when the verdict is read, while all the black people in the balcony (because the main floor of the courthouse was for whites only) react in stunned silence. The bottom floor of the courtroom quickly empties as white men file out, slapping each other on the back in congratulations.

Throughout all the downstairs commotion, the blacks in the balcony remained seated, shocked and deeply disappointed that Tom—now a symbol for anyone with brown skin in their community—was unfairly accused and convicted simply because of his race. Then the camera pans to Atticus. To the only white man who'd behaved honorably that day by insisting that all people deserve to be treated with fairness and dignity regardless of their color or creed. It's obvious by the sag of his shoulders that he's brokenhearted over the verdict. He methodically gathers his papers from the defendant's table, puts them into his briefcase, then turns to walk out of the courtroom. And that's when people in the balcony began standing up. First one by one. Then dozens of them.

A kindly old black pastor taps Atticus's precocious seven-year-old daughter, Jean Louise (nicknamed "Scout"), on the shoulder. Scout has chosen to sit up in the balcony throughout the trial and in that particular moment is plopped on the floor with her tomboyish legs dangling through the balusters. The pastor instructs her firmly but warmly, "Miss Jean Louise, stand up. Your father's passing." She glances up to question him, but once she realizes the entire balcony is standing in deference to her father, her countenance transforms from that of a wary little girl to one whose heart has begun to beat for her daddy. She scrambles quickly to her feet and stretches as tall as she can so as to show her esteem for her father.

I cry every time I watch that scene. Partly because I can so identify with having a gruff, distant dad whom I longed to be close to. And partly because it's such a poignant reminder of how Christians should effectively stand in deference to King Jesus, whom Hebrews depicts as sitting at the right hand of Yahweh:

> And to which of the angels has he ever said, "Sit at my right hand until I make your enemies a footstool for your feet"?

HEBREWS 1:13

In the context of a royal court, "sitting at the right hand" means Jesus sits in the seat of distinction, designating His kingly authority. His seated position also implies that everyone else surrounding the throne is standing in honor of His crown. He is Immanuel—God with Us. He condescended to live in a human body with all of its limitations: He got thirsty in the desert, He cried when His friend Lazarus died, and He bled when soldiers scourged Him with a whip embedded with bits of bone. But let's not forget that Jesus rules alongside God the Father. He is the King of all kings. Therefore, it would behoove us to get up off our rear ends for our reigning Redeemer!

Out of all the psalms quoted in the New Testament, Psalm 110:1 is the most commonly cited. Matthew 22:44; Mark 12:36; Luke 20:42-43; Acts 2:34-35 and Hebrews 1:13 all reference the verse. Plus, Matthew 26:64; Mark 14:62; 16:19; Luke 22:69; Romans 8:34; 1 Corinthians 15:25; Ephesians 1:20; Colossians 3:1; and Hebrews 1:3; 8:1; 10:12 all allude to Psalm 110:1.

> *Why do you think Psalm 110:1 was such a favorite among New Testament writers?*

How would you paraphrase Psalm 110:1 into book or movie title?

What is your favorite angel story in the Bible and why? It can involve a single angel—like when Gabriel appears in Daniel 8:15-26; 9:21-27; and Luke 1:11-38—or it might involve a big ol' angel army like the one depicted in Revelation 5:11.

Based on all you've read so far about angels, draw one. Artistic gifts or a lack thereof don't matter because this rendering doesn't have to go on the wall or the refrigerator, unless you want it to.

Note that 1 Corinthians 15:25 describes Christ's present activity slightly differently than all the "seated" references: "For he must reign until he has put all his enemies under his feet." What might you conclude from the difference?

I'm a firm believer that God created women to be different from the men we all know and love. And since He's sovereign in everything He does and everything He creates, our plentiful emotions and sensory orientation (have you ever met a chick who didn't care about the thermostat?) are divinely wired. Which means it's not just OK that we tend to cry during Hallmark movies, have important sticky notes adhered to pages throughout our Bibles, keep mementos from prom stored in a shoebox in the closet, and get misty-eyed at the mere mention of a glue gun—it's quite possibly ordained!

Since we're different, we're going to finish each session of *Hebrews: The Nearness of King Jesus* with some engage-your-heart homework that will hopefully help us hang on to the divine truths of Hebrews and apply them to our lives. Because our goal isn't to simply accumulate biblical knowledge; it's to start living the gospel—the "good news" of Jesus Christ—out loud!

LIVE THE STORY OUT LOUD

1. *Rent the movie* To Kill a Mockingbird *and watch it with your small group, family, friends, or by yourself sometime between now and week 2 of this Bible study.*

2. *Wherever you're watching the movie, during the courtroom scene in which Scout stands up with her friends to honor Atticus, stand up when they do.*

3. *Make a mental note of how it feels—besides a tad awkward—when you rise to show respect (even though it's only a movie, so you're really just playacting).*

4. *When the movie ends, spend some time in prayer—alone or with whomever you watched* To Kill a Mockingbird*—asking God to give you wisdom in showing Jesus more honor and respect.*

5. *Afterward, write out Psalm 110:1 (in your preferred translation) on an index card and draw a crown above the verse. Put the card on your bathroom mirror, the dashboard of your car, or your computer monitor at work (better still, make several cards and post them in multiple places).*

6. *At least once this week, intentionally add the greeting "Dear King Jesus" or the conclusion "Thank You, King Jesus" out loud as you pray.*

The Old Testament quotations in Hebrews 1:5,13 are bracketed by three rhetorical questions:

1. *For to which of the angels did God ever say, "You are my Son, today I have begotten you"?*

2. *Or again, "I will be to him a father, and he shall be to me a son"?*

3. *And to which of the angels has he ever said, "Sit at my right hand until I make your enemies a footstool for your feet"?*

In verse 14, he ends with a final rhetorical question: "Are they not all ministering spirits sent out to serve for the sake of those who are to inherit salvation?"

Why do you think he used rhetorical questions to make his point?

If you had to distill your faith in Jesus into one rhetorical question, what would it be?

Introducing the Book of Hebrews

Hebrews is an important but often neglected book. We can't be dogmatic about the author, the setting, the date, the readers, or the author's intent because the evidence is sparse. Unlike the other letters in the New Testament, the author does not identify himself or greet his readers. Obviously, the readers knew the author (13:18-25), but neither the text nor tradition of the early church identify him.

The earliest tradition favors Paul as author, but the evidence is neither early nor consistent. Clement of Alexandria said Paul wrote the letter in Hebrew for the Jews and Luke translated it. He thought Paul omitted his name to avoid prejudicing his argument due to opposition to him by the Jews.[1] The problem with this testimony is that Hebrews does not seem to be translation Greek, as Clement proposes, but original Greek. In fact, the writer seems to be accomplished in composing and writing in Greek. Clement may have been speculating on the authorship in an attempt to explain the letter's uncertain origin.

Origen noted the style and grammar of the book was not Paul's, but the thoughts were "not inferior to the acknowledged writings of the apostle." Origen thought the writer of Hebrews took notes on Paul's teaching and wrote the letter. While some thought Clement of Rome and others thought Luke wrote it, according to Origen, "Who wrote the epistle, in truth God knows."[2]

The church in the western part of the empire was much slower to recognize Hebrews and to attribute it to Paul. The earliest western testimony concerning authorship comes from Tertullian, and he attributed the book to Barnabas.[3]

The evidence from the text does not favor Paul. He identified himself in the text of all his letters, and personal references in the letters referred to his associates. In Hebrews, no identification appears and Timothy is the only personal reference in the book (13:23). Most likely, Paul would not have referred to himself as one who received the word about Jesus from "those who heard" (2:3), because in Galatians he insisted that his calling and his gospel came directly from Jesus. In addition, Paul's style and grammar in his letters are different from the style and grammar of Hebrews. Paul's influence on the book probably can be explained best by his influence on the author rather than by his direct influence in the writing.

Extensive use of the details of the tabernacle and of Jewish history demonstrate that the writer of Hebrews was from a Jewish background, or at least familiar with Jewish history. The writer was likely of a Hellenistic background because he used only the Septuagint, the Greek translation of the Hebrew Scripture, in his quotations from the Old Testament. Finally, the writer had a high concept of Jesus similar to Paul's, even though the writer of Hebrews used some titles for Jesus that Paul did not use.

A likely date for the writing of Hebrews: between A.D. 65 and 70.

One reference may indicate the location of the writer, but it is uncertain. In 13:24 (NASB) the writer says, "Those from Italy greet you." The preposition "from" has the basic meaning of "away from," indicating the greeters were formerly in Italy. But the word could indicate that they were currently living in Italy.

If we could identify the writer, we could more easily speculate about his location because many early church leaders became associated with certain areas. Timothy is the only person mentioned in the epistle (13:23). We know from Acts and Paul's letters that Timothy was associated with Paul in the area of Asia Minor, Macedonia, and Corinth. If he remained and was imprisoned there as the text implies, the writer may also have been in the area around the Aegean Sea. Lack of evidence from tradition and the text means questions about the writer's location go unanswered. Natural curiosity makes us want to make definite identities, but we cannot.

The date of Hebrews is limited on the late end by its apparent use in Clement's first letter to the Corinthians. He wrote during the latter part of the first century. If he used Hebrews, as seems apparent, then we must settle on a date before his writing. The major factor in deciding on a date for Hebrews comes from the text itself. The writer referred to the sacrificial system in Judaism as though it were still going on. That system ceased in A.D. 70 at the destruction of Jerusalem and the temple by the Romans. The ending of the sacrificial system would have been a very strong argument to support Jesus' once-for-all sacrifice as superior to the Jewish system. A likely date is sometime between A.D. 65 and 70.

Scholars speculate much about the recipients of Hebrews. Their identity also reflects on the purpose of the writer. The use of the tabernacle as the background for the Jewish sacrifice and the use of the Septuagint by the writer argue against a Palestinian destination.

If Clement of Rome did quote Hebrews in his first letter to the Corinthians,[4] we can conclude that Hebrews was available in Rome before the end of the first century. Our best guess would be that Hebrews was written to a congregation in Rome.

Information in the text gives some characteristics of the congregation and reveals the writer's purpose. He clearly addressed Christians in the book. The congregation was most likely Jewish in background. Some have speculated that the congregation was a mixture of Jews and Jewish Christians worshiping in a synagogue.[5] The people may have been hanging on to Judaism and slow in their response to God's leadership to grow as Christians. Throughout the book, the writer gave warnings about disobedience. We conclude that the purpose was to encourage a Christian congregation, probably in Rome, to move ahead in Christian maturity rather than lagging behind in attachment to Jewish heritage and worship.

The two themes of Hebrews are the sufficiency of Jesus and the obligation of believers.

The themes set forth by the writer of Hebrew are intermingled throughout the book. Two general themes predominate: the sufficiency of Jesus and the obligation of believers.

The sufficiency of Jesus emphasizes that He is greater than all who have gone before Him. The following passages speak of His greatness. He is greater revelation (1:1-3) than: angels (1:4-14; 2:5-18), Moses (3:2-6), Joshua (4:1-11), Aaron (5:1-10), Abraham (6:13–7:10), the Levitical priesthood and the law (7:11-28), the tabernacle and the old covenant (8:1–9:10), and the old sacrificial system (9:11-10:18). Because Jesus is superior, He provides a better ministry to believers. His once-for-all sacrifice makes Him the means for believers to enter God's presence.

Obligation means believers must: not drift (2:1-4), maintain confidence (3:6), not be unbelieving (3:12), hold their assurance (3:14), be diligent to enter God's rest (4:11), hold fast their confession (4:14), draw near with confidence (4:16), grow to maturity (5:11–6:20), draw near to the holy place (10:19-22), hold their confession without wavering (10:23), and stimulate one another to love and good deeds (10:24).

Chapter 11 is a reminder of those through the ages who have been faithful though they did not receive the promise believers have received in Jesus. Chapter 12 and chapter 13 continue the mixture of Jesus' sufficiency and exhortations to faithful obedience to God. The writer concluded with some general greetings in 13:18-25.

Adapted from "Introducing the Book of Hebrews" by Jimmy W. Dukes, Biblical Illustrator, summer 1996, 36–40. For further study, look for "Hebrews: The Nearness of King Jesus Biblical Illustrator Bundle" on lifeway.com/hebrews.

1. Eusebius, Ecclesiastical History, 6.14.
2. Eusebius, 6.25.
3. See Donald Guthrie, New Testament Introduction, 3d ed. (Downers Grove, IL: InterVarsity Press, 1970), 685–98, for a thorough discussion of the early evidence for Hebrews and its authorship.
4. The First Epistle of Clement to the Corinthians, 36:2-6.
5. For those interested in further study on this subject, all of the available New Testament introductions and many commentaries on Hebrews give detailed information on the various views about the identity of the congregations. See also the article, "Introduction to Hebrews," by Dr. R. E. Glaze and his book, No Easy Salvation (Nashville: Broadman Press, 1966).

Therefore we must pay much closer attention to what we have heard, lest we drift away from it. For since the message declared by angels proved to be reliable, and every transgression or disobedience received a just retribution, how shall we escape if we neglect such a great salvation? It was declared at first by the Lord, and it was attested to us by those who heard, while God also bore witness by signs and wonders and various miracles and by gifts of the Holy Spirit distributed according to his will.
HEBREWS 2:1-4 (ESV)

"Drift away" in verse 1 is translated from the Greek word pararreō, *which also means* _____ _____ *or* _____ _____ .

If we aren't _____ _____ _____ *Jesus, there is a powerful* _____ (____ _____) *that is actively working to pull us away from Him.*

Hebrews 2:5-10 (ESV)

Why did he say Jesus is lower than the angels?

Why did he say that Jesus had to become perfect?

*Make perfect—*_____ , *which means "to complete, to finish or to reach a goal."*

_____

_____

_____

_____

_____

_____

Video sessions available for purchase
at www.lifeway.com/hebrews

Since therefore the children share in flesh and blood, he himself likewise partook of the same things, that through death he might destroy the one who has the power of death, that is, the devil, and deliver all those who through fear of death were subject to lifelong slavery. For surely it is not angels that he helps, but he helps the offspring of Abraham. Therefore he had to be made like his brothers in every respect, so that he might become a merciful and faithful high priest in the service of God, to make propitiation for the sins of the people. For because he himself has suffered when tempted, he is able to help those who are being tempted.

HEBREWS 2:14-18 (ESV)

Discussion Questions:

1. *I told about my American Popsicle in London experience this week. What has been an embarrassing moment in which you felt you didn't fit in? How can you relate that experience to the Jewish Christians in Hebrews?*

2. *What stresses, influences, or temptations make the challenge to not drift away difficult for you?*

3. *How does the reality that Jesus made Himself lower than the angels, became a human, and ultimately tasted death for you make you want to respond to Him? Does the image of Jesus voluntarily giving up His freedom to join your captivity change how you feel about Him?*

MOSES GAVE US RULES BUT JESUS GIVES US REST

WALK A MILE IN HEBREW SHOES

I'd like to start the chapter with an important personal qualification: I do not have an abundance of facial hair. Just in case at the end of this anecdote you wonder whether I'm hirsute, I thought it best to clarify matters up front. Mind you, I have had barely noticeable peach fuzz since puberty, which I like to think is God's way of keeping my face warm in the winter. But on to our cautionary tale.

When I was a senior in high school, the Saturday before my senior prom, Mom asked me to clean under the eaves of our back porch. Of course, normal home-improvement people would have used a pressure washer and mild soap, but not us. Nope, my mom thinks full-strength bleach is the answer to pretty much any sanitation situation. Got some mold on your pool deck? Hose that puppy down with industrial-strength bleach! Toddler scribble on your kitchen wall with a Sharpie? Scrub that rascal—the wall, not the child—with industrial-strength bleach. Mulch in the garden looking a little faded? Slosh on some industrial-strength bleach. Remember how the dad in *My Big Fat Greek Wedding* thought Windex could cure anything? Well, that's how my mom feels about Clorox. She just loves the stuff. And the giant white blotches on all her shorts and T-shirts prove her addiction.

Well, that Saturday while I was perched on a ladder, dutifully wiping a bleach-soaked rag back and forth under the eaves, I kept daydreaming about prom. I imagined Keith and me gliding up to the grand entrance of the hotel in our matchy-matchy outfits—me in a shimmering white dress with spaghetti straps and him in a gleaming white tux. I pictured the red rose wrist corsage I knew he'd already ordered for me—in 1981, we called them "wrist-gays," a term that didn't even come up when I Googled it, making me feel like something one would dig up at an archaeological site—and the smart red boutonniere he'd be wearing on his rented lapel. About that time my Clorox-fume-intoxicated mind drifted to what lipstick color I'd wear to prom, and I had this oh-so-regrettable thought: *Hmm, I bet those little wisps of peach fuzz on my upper lip would be absolutely invisible if I put some of Mom's industrial-strength bleach on them and let it soak awhile.*

I don't remember how long I let that bleach burn, but I do remember the consequences: my upper lip was still swollen and scabby for prom night. All the Maybelline in the world couldn't cover up my cosmetic train wreck. And you can bet your bottom dollar I never confused Clorox with Sally Hansen Creme Hair Bleach again. They may sound like the same thing, but the active ingredient in Mom's mulch revitalizer is vastly different than Sally's hair-lightening product and you CAN NOT SUBSTITUTE one for the other.

Some of the Hebrews were making a similar mistake, trying to substitute Moses for Jesus. But they soon learned that Moses, though a heroic leader, couldn't hold a candle to the Light of the World.

LEAN INTO THE STORY

Therefore, holy brothers, you who share in a heavenly calling, consider Jesus, the apostle and high priest of our confession, who was faithful to him who appointed him, just as Moses also was faithful in all God's house. For Jesus has been counted worthy of more glory than Moses—as much more glory as the builder of a house has more honor than the house itself. (For every house is built by someone, but the builder of all things is God.) Now Moses was faithful in all God's house as a servant, to testify to the things that were to be spoken later, but Christ is faithful over God's house as a son. And we are his house if indeed we hold fast our confidence and our boasting in our hope.

HEBREWS 3:1-6

Don't you appreciate it when a parent, spouse, boss, or teacher points out a mistake you've made without implying you're stupid? I got to co-teach a Bible study for years with an incredible mentor named Sue Johnson, who's about twenty years older (and at least fifty years wiser) than I am. I made gobs of mistakes—large theological errors and laughable foot-in-my-mouth ones—while we explored and expounded on the divine love story of Scripture together. But Sue was always so gracious in her "rebuke" that it felt more like a hug than a spanking. Sometimes I didn't even realize she'd corrected me until weeks afterward.

That's basically how the shepherd of Hebrews begins this theological correction too. Before acknowledging their error, he addresses them warmly as "brothers." How kind. He could've said, "You dimwits, if your brain weren't connected to your neck, you'd have lost it by now!" But he didn't.

If you're anything like me, you've probably wondered exactly what defines a "Hebrew." Is it an old-fashioned term for Jewish people? Is it a members-only fraternity that demands a password and a secret handshake? Do they still exist in our culture, and, if so, can we tell who they are by their hairstyle or jersey color? Well, here's the deal: Abraham is the first person called a Hebrew, in Genesis 14:13. His great-great-great-great-great-grandfather was named Eber (Genesis 10:24). Eber means "one who traverses" or "one who crosses over," from which we get the English derivative "Heber" or "Hebrew." Therefore, based on Jewish ancestry, a Hebrew is one descended from Eber, which includes Abraham and his brothers Nahor and Haran. However, since the descendants of Nahor and Haran don't show up later in the Old Testament (likely because they assimilated into other cultural groups), only Abraham and his descendants are still referred to as Hebrews.[1] Some have proposed the name comes from the word "Habiru," which was a derogatory term the Egyptians used to describe the Semitic tribes who wandered throughout the Middle East, tending sheep and goats. But in light of Abraham's genealogy, that term is probably just coincidental.

Instead of shaming his misguided sheep, the pastor of the Hebrews claims them as belonging to his family—"holy brothers"—and part of the tribe he's totally committed to, then he reminds them that they belong to God's family: "you who share in a heavenly calling." In so doing, this tenderhearted spiritual leader effectively wraps his students in a big, ol' encouraging bear hug before he begins to gently correct their misunderstanding about Moses.

What irritates you when someone corrects you?

What words or attitudes make you more willing to accept correction?

Has anyone showed you how to correct with love and affirmation? If so, what did he or she model for you?

Once, while trapped in a moving vehicle on a long road trip, I was confronted by a dear friend about my penchant for gossip. Since I was driving and there were lots of semi-trucks on the interstate that day, I had to keep my eyes focused on the road. So while I bravely kept the SUV in between the lines, she gleefully poked my bruises in air-conditioned comfort. Or so it seemed. When she quoted Proverbs 10:19—"If you talk a lot, you are sure to sin; if you are wise, you will keep quiet" (NCV)—I was tempted to pretend there was a pothole, thereby jerking the wheel and causing her head to whack into the car window. (Mind you, I didn't give in to the temptation!)

But my resentment did begin to boil. *Well, la-tee-dah, Little Miss Perfect. Just who in the heck do you think you are to call me out on loose talk when you've got a great big mouth too? Remember the other day in Target when you commented on how wide that woman's backside was in the checkout line? Maybe you should clue in to the fact that you've got three fingers pointing back at YOU, while you're pointing one at me!*

When there was a break in traffic, I took a deep breath and turned to recount a few choice times when I'd witnessed her gossiping. But when I saw her face, I couldn't go through with my defensive diatribe.

My friend had tears streaming down her cheeks—obviously, it had all but killed her to confront me. She wasn't trying to be right and shove my face in my sin; she was trying to be righteous and help me scoot closer to Jesus.

> *Proverbs 27:6 says, "The wounds of a friend are trustworthy, but the kisses of an enemy are excessive" (HCSB). How have you benefited from a friend who was willing to risk upsetting you to help you scoot closer to Jesus?*

We all know the difference between a gracious, God-honoring rebuke and a shaming, self-righteous ambush. Unfortunately, we tend to preach the former but practice the latter. Under the guise of "confrontation" or "accountability," we sometimes fillet our brothers and sisters, leaving shreds of their heart on the ground. All too often we use hand grenades to point out other people's mistakes, when a scalpel would be sufficient.

The key distinction between recognizing ungodly behavior and passing judgment on others is the posture of our heart. Are we aware of other people's mistakes because they trust us and have confided in us, or have we appointed ourselves the moral police to justify examining blemishes in everyone's behavior? Is our ultimate goal to help restore prodigals to a redemptive relationship with Jesus, or do we secretly aspire to elevate ourselves by condemning those around us?

Since most of us struggle with this confrontation thing, we need to pay attention to how the pastor of Hebrews rolled: he served the truth to his congregation, but not before generously basting it with the sauce of genuine affection.

Read Galatians 6:1. What did it look like the last time you experienced this charge from the apostle Paul? Were you the confronter or the confrontee?

Where would you place yourself on the Comfortable with Confrontation continuum?

1————————————————————————————————10

I always speak the truth, and if it causes some hurt feelings for whiny babies, then too bad.

When I even think about confronting anybody, I lose sleep and sometimes break out in hives.

If you're on the far left of the scale and tend to leave bodies in the wake of your truth-telling, pray for God to help you become more gracious in your confrontations. Consider asking some trusted friends or a Christian counselor to help you in this area. If you're on the far right side, read Matthew 18:15-17. Ask God to help you to better engage in this difficult, yet necessary, arena of reconciliation in the body of Christ.

Surely much to the Hebrews' delight, their pastor still had one more metaphorical bear hug to dole out before getting to the Moses section of the sermon: "consider Jesus, the apostle and high priest of our confession" (Hebrews 3:1b). *Consider Jesus.* In other words, think about our Savior. Focus your attention on our Redeemer. Concentrate on the King of all kings. The simple command to meditate on the Messiah is the answer to every tangled relational web we've ever been caught in, every steep circumstantial hill that has zapped our spiritual and emotional strength, and every deep valley of depression that has left us gasping for hope. *Consider Jesus.*

Stop for just a minute. How does considering Jesus immediately impact some relationship in your life right now?

I went through a very dark night of the soul a few years ago when the death of my dad, the loss of a dear friend, and a cancer diagnosis for me all occurred within the same month. My cancer initially presented as a potentially life-threatening melanoma but turned out to be just a really aggressive (but non-life-threatening) basal-cell carcinoma the doctor carved out of my scalp. The only side effect I had to suffer is that now I can't wear hair-fountains or super high ponytails because my gnarly over-ear scar tends to alarm people and frighten small children.

But the combined onslaught of sorrow and anxiety tackled me to the ground and left me weak with discouragement. All I really wanted to do in the days and weeks that followed Dad's death, my friend's departure, and the cancer biopsy was curl up in bed with a tub of Ben and Jerry's and watch back-to-back episodes of *Duck Dynasty*.

Thinking about Jesus is the only thing that enabled me to put one foot in front of the other instead of pulling the covers over my head and staying in bed. Every morning I woke up feeling sucker punched by the reality that my father, my friend, and a chunk of my head were missing. So I would literally say the name of Jesus out loud several times. Jesus. Jesus. Jesus. Simply focusing on Him for a minute or two gave my feeble heart the boost it needed to beat through another difficult day. Meditating on Christ's sufficiency gave my ricocheting thoughts a safe place to land. Considering Jesus kept me going when I wanted to quit.

> *What caused your last pull-the-covers-over-your-head-and-gobble-ice-cream season?*

What prompted you to ultimately pause and consider Jesus in the midst of your pain?

How often do you speak the name of Jesus out loud during the course of a normal day?

Why do you think we tend to consider Jesus more often in hard seasons than in happy ones?

Spend a few minutes doing what I like to call "divine deep breathing."
Inhale deeply, thinking, "I'm inhaling God's peace." Hold that breath
for several seconds; then exhale as long as you can, thinking, "I'm
exhaling anxiety." After following this deep breathing protocol at least
three times to calm your heart and mind, write down some of your
thoughts about Jesus under the "Consider Jesus" heading below.

CONSIDER JESUS

_____

_____

_____

_____

_____

_____

The most compelling literary feature of Hebrews is the ongoing thesis-styled argument that Jesus is superior to anyone or anything else, as evidenced by the use of the words "better," "more," and "greater," which appear a combined total of twenty-five times in the text. This comparative motif is the main rhetorical strategy in this theological gem.[2]

Now that the Hebrews have been hugged and had their spirits calmed by considering Jesus, their teacher launches into the rectifying-wrong-doctrine part of their lesson with the following rationale. Read Hebrews 3:1-6. Here's my summation of the pastor's line of argument:

- Moses lived faithfully in God's house; Jesus built the house.

- Moses served in God's house; Jesus rules supreme over the house.

- Moses testified to what God would do; Jesus is the revelation of his testimony.

Notice that the pastor doesn't kick Moses to the curb here. As a matter of fact, the deferential treatment with which he recounts Moses' legacy indicates that he's sympathetic to their nostalgia. He understands their longing for the good ol' days when, with God's empowerment, Moses defeated Pharaoh's finest, marched the Israelites across a sandy path that miraculously sliced through the Red Sea, and guffawed the first time God sprinkled them with manna from heaven. He doesn't discount Moses' leadership; he simply clarifies that Moses had clay feet. His bottom line is people don't deserve pedestals.

Read Acts 10:25-26. Have you ever seen someone grovel before a prominent Christian leader as Cornelius did with Peter? If so, how did it make you feel?

Rewrite the motto "People Don't Deserve Pedestals" in your own words.

Why do you think people and pedestals are a bad combination?

Forgive me if the following section gives you whiplash, but we're going to take a quick left turn. While Moses did not deserve a pedestal, he was still a good man who mostly acted with integrity. He treated others with compassion and lived in submission to God's will. Sometimes it bugs me that so many of our modern-day "heroes" are lauded for their physical appearance, rebellious reputation, or number of Twitter followers, as opposed to having upstanding character and strong moral fiber like Moses.

Think about it for a second: little girls look up to reality television stars, even if they wear dental floss disguised as fashion and post videos of their sexual escapades on Facebook. Boys admire professional athletes, even if they have more drug possession and assault charges than they do touchdowns or assists. It seems everyone admires musical artists even if they mumble explicit lyrics, trash hotel rooms for a hobby, and gleefully curse on award shows.

I'm thankful wearing hose in church is no longer de rigueur. I think pantyhose were invented by a spawn of Satan, but I sure wish behaving yourself in the limelight was still in style. Because it seems hooligans with publicists are the most likely to be called heroes in our postmodern culture.

Noted historian and Pulitzer Prize–winning author Daniel J. Boorstin lamented this sad phenomena in an interview several years ago. He said, "Celebrity-worship and hero-worship should not be confused. Yet we confuse them every day, and by doing so we come dangerously close to depriving ourselves of all real models. We lose sight of the men and women who do not seem great because they are famous but are famous because they are great. We come closer and closer to degrading all fame into notoriety."[3] What a great reminder for us to pay closer attention to the people we allow to influence us: the authors we read, the blogs we follow, the sermons we download.

What Christian books are currently on your nightstand? Why does the voice of those particular authors resonate with you?

Which renowned Christian leaders—like Billy Graham or Beth Moore or Rick Warren—do you most admire? How do you differentiate between admiration and worship?

SCOOT YOUR CHAIR A LITTLE CLOSER TO JESUS

Speaking of Moses being a good guy, has it ever bothered you that he didn't make it into the promised land? Now be honest and don't parrot some politically correct Sunday school answer. Because if we're being honest, the majority of us are at least a tad troubled that poor old Moses got the short end of the stick. I know God didn't approve the whole rock-whacking-thus-showing-disrespect incident:

> In the first month, the entire company of the People of Israel arrived in the Wilderness of Zin. The people stayed in Kadesh. Miriam died there, and she was buried. There was no water there for the community, so they ganged up on Moses and Aaron. They attacked Moses: "We wish we'd died when the rest of our brothers died before GOD. Why did you haul this congregation of GOD out here into this wilderness to die, people and cattle alike? And why did you take us out of Egypt in the first place, dragging us into this miserable country? No grain, no figs, no grapevines, no pomegranates—and now not even any water!" Moses and Aaron walked from the assembled congregation to the Tent of Meeting and threw themselves facedown on the ground. And they saw the Glory of GOD. GOD spoke to Moses: "Take the staff. Assemble the community, you and your brother Aaron. Speak to that rock that's right in front of them and it will give water. You will bring water out of the rock for them; congregation and cattle will both drink." Moses took the staff away from GOD's presence, as commanded. He and Aaron rounded up the whole congregation in front of the rock. Moses spoke: "Listen, rebels! Do we have to bring water out of this rock for you?" With that Moses raised his arm and slammed his staff against the rock—once, twice. Water poured out. Congregation and cattle drank. GOD said to Moses and Aaron, "Because you didn't trust me, didn't treat me with holy reverence in front of the People of Israel, you two aren't going to lead this company into the land that I am giving them."

NUMBERS 20:1-12 (THE MESSAGE)

But still, after Moses had led the Israelites through the wilderness for forty long years, to ban him from Canaan seems pretty harsh. I mean, good night, if I'd been the one leading those complaining stinkers, I would've been smacking them upside the head instead of simply hitting a stone. Now, before you shut this workbook and brand me a heretic, please know I'm not doubting God's sovereignty. It's just that this is one of those His-ways-are-higher-than-ours (Isaiah 55:9) situations when my dinky human noggin doesn't comprehend God's action plan. From my perspective, it seems like it would've been enough to make Moses write "I will not whack rocks" on a chalkboard fifty times.

What about you? Have you struggled with some situation in which God seemed less than fair in His treatment of you or someone you care about? Tell me about it.

One day when I was studying in Starbucks—one of my favorite places to sprawl out with my Bible and a couple of commentaries, because I've had some awesome conversations with curious-about-God strangers there—I paused at a passage I've read at least a hundred times before:

> Six days later, Jesus took Peter, James, and John, the brother of James, up on a high mountain by themselves. While they watched, Jesus' appearance was changed; his face became bright like the sun, and his clothes became white as light. Then Moses and Elijah appeared to them, talking with Jesus.

MATTHEW 17:1-3 (NCV)

It's the story about the Mount of Transfiguration, wherein the three men closest to Jesus—Peter, James, and John—hike with Him up a hill on the north side of the Sea of Galilee. When they get to the top—*SHAZAM!*—the Son of God begins to glow. Then right about the time this trembling trio of gobsmacked disciples picks their chins up off the ground, two more shiny guys (who'd been dead a very long time) miraculously appear and start chatting with the Messiah (by the way, I would so need some serious counseling if I observed shimmery, gabby, formerly dead people).

Not until I was perusing this colorful story for the umpteenth time in that coffee shop did I have a smack-yourself-on-the-forehead-like-on-the-V8-commercial epiphany: the Mount of Transfiguration was not only in the middle of the promised land, it was probably one of the most scenic views overlooking the entire Sea of Galilee … and there stood dear Moses right next to Jesus. So he did make it to the land of milk and honey after all.

Now picture Moses on Oprah's couch. He's fidgeting in his Birkenstocks until she asks him the zinger question of the interview: "Moses, if you had the choice of walking into the promised land with several million sweaty, complaining people—most of whom had gotten on your last nerve during your natural life—OR waiting to set foot in the promised land until it was God's perfect timing and getting to rub shoulders with Jesus, which would you choose?" You know he'd pull a Tom Cruise and jump on the couch, shouting, "The second option, Oprah! The one where I get to be with my Savior!"

Make a list of some things that seemed or seem extremely important at the time but will lose their significance when you're with Jesus in His completed kingdom.

Why do you suppose we have such difficulty keeping a kingdom perspective when we encounter difficulties here on earth?

We so easily assume God is being too harsh or unfair when life isn't turning out quite the way we hoped it would. We humans have a tendency to think our Creator Redeemer is bound by the same parameters of time and space that confine our mortal bodies. But He isn't. He is infinitely bigger and better than our understanding. His love for us extends far beyond our ability to imagine. His perfect plan is to give us a hope and a future (Jeremiah 29:11). He really will work everything out for our good and His glory (Romans 8:28); it just might not be on our timetable.

So in this in-between time, when it's tempting to search for a human "hero" we can see instead of one we can't, consider Jesus. And rest in the fact that, one day, we'll get to stand next to His radiance too.

LIVE THE STORY OUT LOUD

1. *Get a sheet of blue paper and red paper and cut both sheets into fourths.*

2. *On each blue square, write a different unmet desire that has made you sad (e.g., a prodigal child or spouse, infertility, a broken relationship, etc.).*

3. *On each red square, write an event that made you really mad (e.g., a cheating spouse, physical/emotional/sexual abuse, a betrayal, etc.).*

4. *Roll all eight slips of paper into tiny scrolls and secure them with rubber bands.*

5. *Find an old rock or brick wall with noticeable gaps (it would obviously behoove you to have a wall like this on your property). When you find it, shove your wee scrolls into the crevices in the same way people jam prayers into the Wailing Wall in Jerusalem.*

6. *Pray something like Jesus' prayer of submission prior to the cross—"not my will, but yours, be done" (Luke 22:42)—while filling those holes with the scribbled cries of your heart.*

EXTRA CREDIT FOR BIBLE NERDS:

Read the Book of Deuteronomy, which is the conclusion of the Pentateuch (the first five books of the Bible) and contains the two farewell speeches Moses gave the Israelites before he died and was buried on Mount Nebo (in present-day Jordan in a grave no archaeologist has ever found), and count how many times he uses the word "remember."

"BETTER" IN HEBREWS

When we say "better," we imply some scale of comparison. The context determines what is being measured. For instance, if we say one race horse is "better" than another, we could mean "faster" (though any number of other scales might be implied, such as "prettier" or "more expensive").

In the context of comparing people, the understanding may not be a particular attribute but may denote status, for example, "a slave is not greater than his master" (John 13:16, HCSB). The writer of the Book of Hebrews uses the Greek word *kreitton* (sometimes translated as "better, superior, greater, or mightier") in both senses—as attribute and status. The word functions as the comparative of *agathos* (translated "good").[1] The writer of Hebrews shows comparisons in other ways, but this is by far his favorite. Of the 20 New Testament occurrences of *kreitton*, 13 are in Hebrews.[2]

Hebrews opens with an idea of contrast—in earlier days God spoke in a variety of ways by the prophets, but in these last days He has spoken by His Son. In the Greek this long initial sentence runs from 1:1-4, wherein the writer gave "seven affirmations describing the Son's person, work, and current status."[3] In the last of the list, the author declared that the Son has become superior *(kreitton)* to the angels as His inherited name is more excellent than theirs (v. 4).

Likely, the early readers easily made the connection between the prophets and the angels since, in Jewish thinking, both played a role in delivering God's message in the previous age.[4] Jesus is greater than the angels by His status as Son, the ultimate Messenger. Angels worship Him (v. 6), not vice versa. In fact, Hebrews describes angels as ministering spirits sent to serve those who will inherit salvation (v. 14). God subjected the world to the Son, not to angels. Through the incarnation the Son was made lower than the angels for only a time, after which He was highly exalted over everything (2:5-9).

Jesus' priesthood is superior because He is eternal.

Jesus as our High Priest is a central teaching of Hebrews. But the author did not begin with the idea of contrast but of comparison. He showed the similarities between Jesus and the priests of the Jews—selected from among men (5:1), able to sympathize with our weaknesses (4:14-15), and not self-appointed but called by God (5:4-5). Then the author used comparison: Jesus was sinless (4:15; 7:26); He traveled through the heavens (4:14; 7:26; 9:11); and He is the source of eternal salvation (5:9). He indeed is our great High Priest (4:14).

Another characteristic feature of Hebrews is the author's discussion of the high priestly order of Melchizedek (5:6,10; 6:20; 7:1-22). The contrast begins between Melchizedek (the greater, *kreitton,* 7:7), who received the tenth and gave the blessing, and Abraham (the lesser), who gave the tenth and received the blessing. Thus even the priesthood of Aaron and the Levites was inferior to Melchizedek, since they are descendants of Abraham and corporately a part of him. But the real point is to show Jesus within the line of Melchizedek's priesthood and so superior to Aaron and the Levitical priesthood. In Christ, the priesthood changed (v. 12). His priesthood is superior because He is eternal (vv. 16-17,24-25), and unlike anyone else, He became a priest by God's oath (vv. 20-21). He is holy, blameless, pure, and does not need to make sacrifices for Himself as all other priests do. He is also unique in that He offered Himself as the sacrifice, once for all, unlike all other sacrifices that needed to be repeated over and over again (vv. 26-28; 9:12,26-28).

The word *kreitton* also appears in one of the warning passages in Hebrews. Although some might turn away from God, the author was confident of "better" things concerning his readers and their ability to persevere in the way of salvation (6:9).

With the establishment of Jesus as our great High Priest, a better *(kreitton)* hope has now been introduced through which we are able to draw near to God (7:19). Because God stands behind His appointment, sealed by His own oath, Jesus is the guarantee of a better *(kreitton)* covenant (v. 22). The author expanded the idea of the better *(kreitton)* covenant (8:6) by quoting Jeremiah 31:31-34 and by declaring the old covenant obsolete and soon to disappear (Heb. 8:7-13). Jesus is the mediator of this new covenant, and His covenant ministry takes place in the true, heavenly sanctuary. Jesus' covenant is superior *(kreitton)* to those who serve in a mere copy or shadow of the one in heaven (8:6,2-5; 9:15).

The contrast between the earthly and heavenly tabernacles as well as the difference between

Christ's sacrifice and the blood of animal sacrifices continue in chapter 9, punctuated in verse 23 with another occurrence of *kreitton*. As suitable as it was for the earthly tabernacle to be purified by shed blood because of the sins of the Israelites, so also the heavenly things were purified, but with a "superior builder" (11:10, HCSB). Abel's blood bore witness to Cain's guilt and sin (Gen. 4:10), but Christ's blood speaks of better *(kreitton)* things (12:24). He "has won our forgiveness, 'crying out' that people of the new covenant are no longer guilty, having been cleansed completely from sin."[5]

Christ came the first time to sacrifice His life for the sin of the world. The next time He comes will be to bring salvation in its fullness and completion to those who await Him (9:28). The first readers of Hebrews had already suffered considerably as Christians (10:32-34). They were able to withstand even the loss of personal property because better *(kreitton)* and lasting possessions would be theirs on that day (v. 34). In this way they were following the example of the saints who had gone before them in search of a city built by God (11:10; 13:14) and a better *(kreitton)* land, which was heavenly as opposed to earthly (11:16). God has prepared something better *(kreitton)* for us together, both the living saints and those who have already passed away (v. 40). Resisting the pleasures and temptations of this world, while standing firm in our faith, we must set our hope on that better *(kreitton)* resurrection, even in the face of persecution (v. 35).

In a pluralistic society that exalts tolerance, the idea of one faith system being "better" than another is not so readily accepted. In the Book of Hebrews we see that God's activity among the children of Israel was not wrong or bad but was preparatory for what was to come. With the arrival of Christ, the former was superseded by the "better." By extension, the priesthood of Christ is superior to any other means of approaching God. In fact, it is only by Christ's atoning work that we can draw near to God. From an eternal perspective, the believer looks forward to better things to come—when Christ returns. That should motivate us to hold firmly to our faith and to run with endurance the race that lies before us until that day we enter the eternal city not made with the hands of men.

> In a pluralistic society that exalts tolerance, the idea of one faith system being "better" than another is not so readily accepted.

Adapted from "'Better' in Hebrews" by Steve Booth, Biblical Illustrator, *fall 2006, 19–21. For further study, look for "Hebrews: The Nearness of King Jesus Biblical Illustrator Bundle" on* lifeway.com/hebrews.

1. Walter Bauer, William F. Arndt, and F. Wilbur Gingrich, A Greek-English Lexicon of the New Testament and Other Early Christian Literature, 3d ed. (Chicago: The University of Chicago Press, 1957), 450-451.
2. The occurrences of kreitton *outside Hebrews are 1 Corinthians 7:9,38; 11:17; 12:31; Philippians 1:23; 1 Peter 3:17; 2 Peter 2:21.*
3. George H. Guthrie, Hebrews in The NIV Application Commentary (Grand Rapids: Zondervan, 1998), 47.
4. William Lane, Hebrews 1–8, Word Biblical Commentary, vol. 47a (Dallas: Word Books, 1991), 37–38. See Hebrews 2:2, "the message spoken by angels." Also Acts 7:38,53; Galatians 3:19.
5. Guthrie, 422

Two key Christological concepts ...

The _____ and the _____ of Jesus.

Hebrews was preached as a _____ .

It is critical for Christians to actively move toward Jesus. Why?

Hebrews 4:4 refers to _____ rest.

Hebrews 4:6-7 refers to _____ rest.

Hebrews 4:8 refers to _____ rest.

Hebrews 4:9-10 refers to _____ rest.

1. God _____ rest.

2. God _____ rest _____ the fall.

Rest is God's merciful _____ for our _____ .

Hebrews 4:11-13 (ESV)

God's Word reveals what is going on in us, both the _____ of our hands and the _____ of our heart.

Matthew 11:28-30 (The Message)

Video sessions available for purchase
at www.lifeway.com/hebrews

Discussion Questions:

1. *In what ways do you think you have tried to substitute something for Jesus? Did it work as poorly as my bleach substitute?*

2. *How has God shown you that He is watching over you and you can rest in Him?*

3. *How has God had you stay in a difficult time rather than be rescued?*

4. *Has anyone showed you how to correct with love and affirmation? If so, what did he or she model for you?*

_____

_____

_____

_____

_____

_____

_____

_____

_____

_____

_____

_____

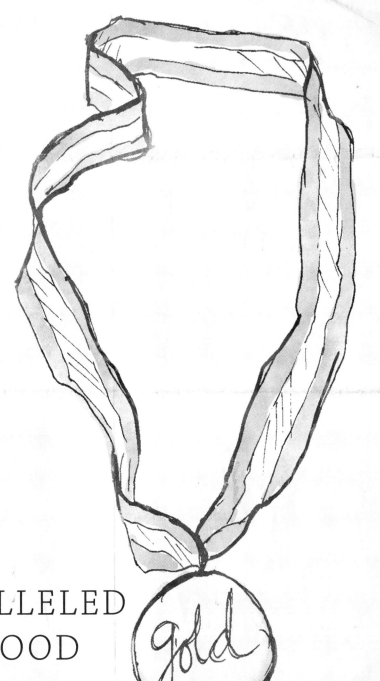

WEEK 3

AN UNPARALLELED PRIESTHOOD

WALK A MILE IN HEBREW SHOES

Ginny Bishop and Brenda Brown were my best friends growing up. Brenda is also my second cousin, so I suppose our moms would've forced the relationship on us regardless. But we really did like each other. Ginny is one of five sisters, so being a good girlfriend comes naturally to her.

From the glitter-and-glue days of elementary school through the rapture and rupture of high school, the three of us remained an invincible, inseparable team. Not unlike the cool cats on *The Mod Squad* or the gorgeous heroines of *Charlie's Angels* … at least, that's how we imagined it.

My favorite memories from our triune kinship center on the mock Olympic gymnastic competitions we frequently staged in Ginny's front yard. Ginny would pop one of her parents' classical music tapes into a boom box. Then the contest would officially begin with as much pomp and circumstance as we could manage with whatever household items we scrounged up. We especially liked prancing around with the multicolored scarves that served as the flag of whatever fictional country each of us represented. After the stirring opening ceremonies, we made a corporate decision regarding the sequence of our presentations. Then we each took a turn performing an extemporaneous routine for the other two to judge.

While all three of us were athletically inclined, none of us had ever taken gymnastics lessons. Much like the auditions of tone-deaf contestants on *American Idol,* our performances were infused with great enthusiasm but were a bit thin on the technical side. However, I truly believe our lack of formal training propelled us to new artistic heights. For example, since I never quite mastered the compulsory back handspring, I often used the Japanese plum tree at the edge of the lawn as a prop. I reasoned that incorporating a few graceful swings from its lower branches should earn big points for creativity.

What's one of the craziest things you did just for fun when you were a kid? (Think riding your banana-seat bicycle through the fog that spewed out from the mosquito truck. Doing cannonballs off the dock into a freezing-cold lake. Calling perfect strangers on the phone and asking if their refrigerator's running, then squealing, "Well, you'd better catch it before it runs out the door!" and hanging up in a paroxysm of giggles.)

Did you tend to be a conformist or nonconformist when you were growing up? How about now?

Share a habit or hobby others might consider unconventional.

Do you think a little unconventionality could actually be a positive trait in a Christian's personality? If so, explain how.

I can't help but laugh when I recall our final competition after years of hurling our bodies about in what we convinced ourselves were routines any amateur gymnast would be proud to call her own. Having come to the realization that none of our other high school friends spent hours rolling around in the grass for grins, we finally agreed that it was time to hang up our ratty leotards for good. But we wanted to go out on a high note, so we began dreaming up one last glorious event. We planned the finale for weeks, taking care to make sure our routines were flawless and our outfits as tacky as possible.

When the appointed afternoon arrived, Ginny blasted the Bach a bit louder than usual, and we paraded across her yard with more panache than ever for the opening ceremonies. Cars actually slowed down to watch the spectacle. Granted, their voyeurism was partly fueled by the fact that Ginny's house was on a scenic boulevard where drivers tended to poke along, admiring the stately old homes. And most of them probably assumed that our sporting melodrama was something the neighborhood association had sponsored for their entertainment, like an outdoor concert or a chili cook-off.

However, they did seem to sense this particular show was the end of an era, because as the contest wore on, a few drivers pulled over to the edge of the road and began to honk their horns and yell support out their windows. Unfortunately, horn toots and a few catcalls were the only prizes we received for our silly aerobics exercise since our exhibition was not officially sanctioned by the Olympic Committee. Frankly, I'm thinking even a preschool tumbling class wouldn't have claimed us because we weren't real gymnasts. We were just limber teenagers playing around—an anemic shadow of the athletic substance that fills television screens across the world every four years.

This week we'll see that the pastor of Hebrews was trying to teach his sheep that the priests who facilitated worship in the temple were only a shadow of the substance of Jesus Christ. They were mostly good men, doing their best to help God's people practice and apply their faith, but they weren't the real light of the world. The feeble illumination of the priesthood was like a single match compared to the supernova brilliance of Jesus Christ.

LEAN INTO THE STORY

Over and over again, you'll hear the pastor of Hebrews talking about the priesthood, because that was the mental and emotional hyphen the Jews had between themselves and God. The priesthood had been their only tangible connection to the Creator for centuries; therefore, their spiritual leader had to show them that Jesus fulfilled everything the human priests before Him had failed to do. The pastor continues to remind his congregation that Jesus cared for them in a way their priests could not:

> Since we have a great high priest, Jesus the Son of God, who has gone into heaven, let us hold on to the faith we have. For our high priest is able to understand our weaknesses. He was tempted in every way that we are, but he did not sin. Let us, then, feel very sure that we can come before God's throne where there is grace. There we can receive mercy and grace to help us when we need it.

HEBREWS 4:14-16 (NCV)

Imagine what comfort those words brought to the adulterer who deeply regretted cheating on the love of his life or the woman who wore jealousy like a heavy chain around her neck because her sister had a dozen kids and she was infertile? Jesus knows the tormented thoughts in the darkest corner of their heart, but instead of turning away in disgust, He turns toward them with empathetic kindness. Instead of getting the whipping they deserve at God's throne, they are told to expect an embrace, because Jesus has already taken the beating. Good night, when I stop and think about that exchange of guilt for grace, my eyes brim with gratitude now.

> *Imagine the darkest, vilest thought you've had or deed you've done. Now try to imagine Jesus standing beside you at the exact moment of your transgression. What expression do you picture on His face? Why?*

Read 2 Corinthians 5:21. What sin do you most regret God assigning to Christ's resume, so that you could be pronounced "righteous"?

After leading with the sufficient kindness of Christ, the author shifts to gently point out the insufficiency of the priesthood:

> [1]Every high priest is chosen from among other people. He is given the work of going before God for them to offer gifts and sacrifices for sins. [2]Since he himself is weak, he is able to be gentle with those who do not understand and who are doing wrong things. [3]Because he is weak, the high priest must offer sacrifices for his own sins and also for the sins of the people.

HEBREWS 5:1-3 (NCV)

What strength of the human priesthood does verse 2 highlight?

What weakness of the human priesthood does verse 3 highlight?

How does Jesus incorporate the strength without any of the weakness?

The Hebrews were very familiar with the Old Testament. For generations they'd been taught about how God established the priesthood as a means of mediating worship soon after Moses had led their great-great-and-then-some grandparents out of Egypt, away from that hateful pharaoh toward the land of promise:

"You are to command the Israelites to bring you pure oil from crushed olives for the light, in order to keep the lamp burning continually. In the tent of meeting outside the veil that is in front of the testimony, Aaron and his sons are to tend the lamp from evening until morning before the LORD. This is to be a permanent statute for the Israelites throughout their generations. Have your brother Aaron, with his sons, come to you from the Israelites to serve Me as priest—Aaron, his sons Nadab and Abihu, Eleazar and Ithamar."

EXODUS 27:20-28:1 (HCSB)

They were also definitely familiar with the priesthood blooper reel, which revealed how not too long after God appointed Moses' brother to be the lead Jewish gymnast—oops, I mean the high priest of Israel—Aaron made a doozy of a mistake:

When the people saw that Moses delayed in coming down from the mountain, they gathered around Aaron and said to him, "Come, make us a god who will go before us because this Moses, the man who brought us up from the land of Egypt—we don't know what has happened to him!"

Then Aaron replied to them, "Take off the gold rings that are on the ears of your wives, your sons, and your daughters and bring them to me." So all the people took off the gold rings that were on their ears and brought them to Aaron. He took the gold from their hands, fashioned it with an engraving tool, and made it into an image of a calf.

EXODUS 32:1-4A (HCSB)

Have you ever done something in ministry that pleased people but may not have pleased God? If so, explain without unduly embarrassing yourself.

Why is allowing people-pleasing to guide our actions particularly dangerous?

Then they said, "Israel, this is your God, who
brought you up from the land of Egypt!"

When Aaron saw this, he built an altar before it.

EXODUS 32:4B-5A (HCSB)

*When Aaron started to shape the calf, do you suppose he thought he
would wind up substituting a calf altar for the altar of God?*

If you were Aaron, how would you have rationalized your actions?

*How do our bad decisions compound themselves and take us places we
never thought we'd go?*

Then he [Aaron] made an announcement: "There will be a festival
to the LORD tomorrow." Early the next morning they arose,
offered burnt offerings, and presented fellowship offerings.
The people sat down to eat and drink, then got up to play.

EXODUS 32:5B-6

What do you suppose these Israelites were thinking?
□ *God will really be pleased with us.*
□ *Wish we were back in Egypt.*
□ *We really liked those earrings Aaron melted down.*
□ *Now this is real worship!*
□ *Your thoughts …*

"This is truly a dark moment for Israel. Moses left Aaron and Hur in charge forty days ago, and both men are beginning to feel the strain. The people are stuck in the desert, and they are growing increasingly impatient without Moses and direction from God. So the people begin to question, and eventually they demand a physical representation of God like the ones their neighbors have. Aaron complies. With Moses and God occupied, the people begin breaking the Ten Directives, one after another: worshiping other gods, making idols, invoking God's name for their own selfish purposes, and committing other indecent acts. The people of God fall quickly, and they fall hard. For a brief period, their very survival is in doubt."[1]

> *How have you observed the reality that sometimes the people of God fall quickly and they fall hard?*

God told Moses to go down the mountain because the people had corrupted themselves. They had quickly turned from obeying God's commands to worshipping the golden calf. Therefore God declared:

> "I have seen this people, and they are indeed a stiff-necked people.
> Now leave Me alone, so that My anger can burn against them and
> I can destroy them. Then I will make you into a great nation."

EXODUS 32:9-10 (HCSB)

> *How would you have responded to the offer to abandon the people who had made your life so difficult and to become the founder of a great new nation of people?*

I probably couldn't have gotten rid of those complainers quickly enough. But we're looking at what made Moses the great leader he was. See how The Message tells the rest of the story.

> [11]Moses tried to calm his GOD down. He said, "Why, GOD, would you
> lose your temper with your people? Why, you brought them out of Egypt

in a tremendous demonstration of power and strength. [12]Why let the Egyptians say, 'He had it in for them—he brought them out so he could kill them in the mountains, wipe them right off the face of the Earth.' Stop your anger. Think twice about bringing evil against your people! [13]Think of Abraham, Isaac, and Israel, your servants to whom you gave your word, telling them 'I will give you many children, as many as the stars in the sky, and I'll give this land to your children as their land forever.'"

[14]And GOD did think twice. He decided not to do the evil he had threatened against his people.

[15]Moses turned around and came down from the mountain, carrying the two tablets of The Testimony. The tablets were written on both sides, front and back. [16]God made the tablets and God wrote the tablets—engraved them.

[17]When Joshua heard the sound of the people shouting noisily, he said to Moses, "That's the sound of war in the camp!"

[18]But Moses said,

> Those aren't songs of victory,
> And those aren't songs of defeat,
> I hear songs of people throwing a party.

[19]And that's what it was. When Moses came near to the camp and saw the calf and the people dancing, his anger flared. He threw down the tablets and smashed them to pieces at the foot of the mountain. [20]He took the calf that they had made, melted it down with fire, pulverized it to powder, then scattered it on the water and made the Israelites drink it.

[21]Moses said to Aaron, "What on Earth did these people ever do to you that you involved them in this huge sin?"

[22]Aaron said, "Master, don't be angry. You know this people and how set on evil they are. [23]They said to me, 'Make us

gods who will lead us. This Moses, the man who brought us out of Egypt, we don't know what's happened to him.'

²⁴"So I said, 'Who has gold?' And they took off their jewelry and gave it to me. I threw it in the fire and out came this calf."

EXODUS 32:5B-24 (THE MESSAGE)

So, basically, after the ancient Israelites decide Moses' tête-à-tête with the Creator of the Universe is taking too long, Aaron morphs from a spiritual giant into a spineless wimp and gives in when they throw a hissy fit and demand an idol. He creates the first cash-for-gold franchise, supervises the kiln while the idol is cooking, and then plans an idol-inauguration party complete with a disco ball and dance floor. But when Moses comes stomping down from Mt. Sinai to confront his brother, Aaron throws the people he's "leading" under the bus and stammers, "It's all their fault! They threw their Rolexes at me, which ricocheted into the bonfire. Then—*SHAZAM!*—out popped a golden calf I had absolutely nothing to do with!"

Do you notice that from the very beginning of the priesthood, it was a bit wobbly? Although I'm not sure how enthused the Hebrews were to admit their ancestors were such fools.

How does it make you feel when you read news reports about a national spiritual leader (like a television evangelist or megachurch pastor) taking a moral tumble?

Read James 3:1 and 1 Timothy 3:1-7. Although these verses seem to mandate a higher level of responsibility for spiritual leaders, theologian D. A. Carson notes (regarding the 1 Timothy passage), "With the exception of only two qualifications [3:2 and 3:6], everything else in this list is elsewhere mandated of all Christians."[2]

So why do you think Christians tend to put pastors and priests on pedestals and then become outraged if they fall?

Unfortunately, the priesthood didn't seem to learn much from its mistakes either because 1 Samuel describes a couple of priests who couldn't contain themselves at all-you-can-eat buffets and no longer craved intimacy with God:

> Now Eli's sons were evil men; they did not care about the LORD. This is what the priests would normally do to the people: Every time someone brought a sacrifice, the meat would be cooked in a pot. The priest's servant would then come carrying a fork that had three prongs. He would plunge the fork into the pot or the kettle. Whatever the fork brought out of the pot belonged to the priest. But this is how they treated all the Israelites who came to Shiloh to offer sacrifices. Even before the fat was burned, the priest's servant would come to the person offering sacrifices and say, "Give the priest some meat to roast. He won't accept boiled meat from you, only raw meat."
>
> If the one who offered the sacrifice said, "Let the fat be burned up first as usual, and then take anything you want," the priest's servant would answer, "No, give me the meat now. If you don't, I'll take it by force."
>
> The Lord saw that the sin of the servants was very great because they did not show respect for the offerings made to the LORD.
>
> 1 SAMUEL 2:12-17 (NCV)

Eli's sons, Hophni and Phinehas, were commissioned as "junior priests" and were taught to treat Israelite meat sacrifices with reverence according to Jewish ceremonial laws. And while, as full-time temple employees, they were allowed a portion of the meat offered for sacrifice, they were supposed to receive it through a sort of holy "potluck" system, wherein they stabbed a big fork into a vat of boiling oil and whatever it brought up was what they got to eat. But these piggy priests decided to boycott the fondue system and began aggressively accosting worshippers before they entered the temple, demanding their steaks up front. Instead of humbly bowing to Yahweh's rules regarding worship, they set up a barbecue pit in the churchyard and demanded prime cuts.

So God warns their dad, Eli, who was serving as the high priest of Israel at the time (the same guy who mentored Samuel, so surely he had some good qualities—although parental discipline doesn't seem to be one of them) about allowing his sons to be such self-centered gluttons: "So why don't you respect the sacrifices and gifts? You honor your

sons more than me. You grow fat on the best parts of the meat the Israelites bring to me"
(1 Samuel 2:29).

It's really interesting that the Hebrew word "honor" used in this warning also means
"to give weight to" or to "be weighty"—that makes it a divine double entendre, under-
scoring the fact that Eli and his boys were getting pudgy from all the marbled meat they
were consuming. As a result of ignoring God's food rules, Eli's and his boys' cholesterol
shot up and they had to start buying their priestly garments at the Big and Tall men's
shop. Ultimately Hophni and Phinehas died young (on the same day, just as God warned
in 1 Samuel 2:34) due to their rebellion, and poor old Eli got so chunky that he fell off a
chair and broke his neck (1 Samuel 4:12-18).

Now to be sure, there were a few faithful priests in the lineage of Levi who led Israel with
humility and dignity. Some of them didn't deejay at idol-dances or gobble up the altar
sacrifices. But still, none of them was perfect. One has to wonder what kept the Hebrews
so dedicated to their priesthood, since all too often their robe-clad spiritual leaders
executed belly flops instead of swan dives.

What would the people closest to you describe you as "craving"?

*On the scale of 1 (disinterested) to 10 (famished), how hungry for
God would you describe yourself as being this season?*

1————————————————————————————————10
Disinterested   Famished

*What circumstances or emotions have triggered your appetite for God
in the past?*

*Read Psalm 63:3-7. If you were paraphrasing this psalm as a personal
prayer, what food would you list as being less satisfying than God
(verse 5)?*

SCOOT YOUR CHAIR A LITTLE CLOSER TO JESUS

When we were growing up, my sweet mama was emphatic about making sure her brood ate healthy food. She used olive oil long before it was considered cool; she asked the butcher for the leanest cuts of meat; she refused to stock our pantry with chips, cookies, or Cokes like the rest of my friends' moms did; and she tried to instill in us the belief that fast food is from the Devil (an idea that evaporated from my mind like a dewdrop on a hot summer's day the minute I left for college). For a few years, she even gave up her beloved iced tea after reading about the dangers of caffeine in one of her health food journals and decided that diluted apple juice with fresh lemon would taste exactly like the sweet tea she'd become famous for (at least at our family reunions).

The rest of our little clan on Valencia Street—Dad Angel, Theresa, John Price, and me—begged her to stop serving watered-down cider at dinner and to resume brewing the yummy tea we were accustomed to, but she refused. She was steadfast in her belief that we would eventually grow to accept weak apple juice with a wedge of citrus hovering feebly on the side of the glass as a substitute for tea. But we never did. We just learned to sip sparingly, like suburban camels. To this day the smell of apple juice makes me a little nauseated.

The priesthood was the dominant theme in Israel's history after God established it through Aaron. While prophets' messages could be difficult to decipher and kings could be defeated, the priesthood had consistently been the Israelites' connection—albeit wobbly—to their Creator. It was the only tangible go-between they had through which to approach God. They brought worship and sacrificial offerings to the temple—a bag of wheat, a jar of olive oil, a lamb or a cow—and the priests prepared those gifts according to ceremonial law, then officially presented the offering to Yahweh. Although as previously discussed, some priests were prone to taking a bite first.

But the Levitical system was innately flawed—as poor a substitute as watered-down apple juice, if I may—because it was innately human. People aren't adequate stand-ins for the Son of God. Jesus Christ is the only priest capable of fulfilling the redemption God promised His people:

And because his obedience was perfect, he was able to give eternal salvation to all who obey him.

HEBREWS 5:9 (NCV)

I'd love to see the faces of those precious first-century Christians when their pastor explained that Jesus was both their perfect High Priest and the perfect sacrifice. I bet it blew their mental hard drive. I mean, what student dares to dream of a professor taking the final exam the student thought she'd have to suffer through? Especially when the student was destined to fail? God didn't lower the standard of moral perfection so we could justify ourselves with mediocre behavior; instead, He chose to meet the standard for us through Jesus. Hallelujah! What a Savior!

LIVE THE STORY OUT LOUD

1. *Rent the movie* Luther, *starring Joseph Fiennes, and watch it with your small group, family, friends, or by yourself sometime between now and week 4 of this study.*

2. *Afterward, write one renewed commitment you're making to Jesus, our perfect High Priest, on a note or index card. Then tape that note on your bedroom door (since the actual Wittenberg door was burned up in a fire in 1760) and tap a finger on it every time you walk in and out of your room this week to remember your promise.*

MOSES IN THE BOOK OF HEBREWS

The writer of Hebrews used the greatness of Moses to build a case for the superior greatness of Jesus. R. Kent Hughes observed that Moses towered over all other Hebrews as the greatest man in their history. Five points of emphasis communicate how Moses stood head and shoulders above all others in the Old Testament. God appointed him as deliverer of His people (Ex. 7–12); Israel's greatest speaking prophet (Num. 12:6-8); law-giver (Ex. 19–20); and Israel's greatest historian (Gen. 1–Deut. 34). Finally, Moses also demonstrated more humility than anyone on the face of the earth (Num. 12:3). So Hughes rightfully titled Moses "The Great Apostle and High Priest of the Old Testament."[1]

Hebrews first refers to Moses in 3:1–4:16 to uphold him, and by comparison, to show the ultimate superiority of Christ. The writer used the literary device of switching back and forth between expositional material about Jesus and exhortations intended to call his audience to faithfulness. But he did not mention Moses until he delivered the main exhortation: "Therefore, holy brothers and companions in a heavenly calling, consider Jesus, the apostle and high priest of our confession; He was faithful to the One who appointed Him, just as Moses was in all God's household" (3:1-2, HCSB).

> God sent both Moses and Jesus to proclaim God's name.

Only in the Book of Hebrews do we find Jesus' title "apostle and high priest." Together the terms form a phrase of tremendous significance. Those who heard this sermon would have undoubtedly thought of Moses' apostolic and priestly functions when God "sent" him as God's representative to deliver His people from bondage in Egypt. God sent both Moses and Jesus to proclaim God's name. Hebrews does not intend, however, to cheapen Moses by the comparison; rather, the intention is to highlight the special status of Christ.[2]

Some veins of Jewish history viewed Moses so highly that they thought of the coming Messiah as a "new Moses."[3] Luke picked up this idea in his account of the transfiguration (Luke 9:28-36). He alone recorded the content of the conversation between Jesus, Moses, and Elijah: "They spoke about his departure [Greek: exodos], which he was about to bring to fulfillment at Jerusalem" (a reference to His death; v. 31, NIV). God sent both Jesus and Moses, and both were faithful to Him. Both delivered God's people—Moses from physical bondage, Jesus from spiritual bondage. In Hebrews 3:2, the phrase "just as" (Greek: hōs kai) levels the two for the moment—but only in comparison to each other's faithfulness to their respective tasks of ministry. Of course, Jesus performed His ministry flawlessly, while Moses made several crucial mistakes. But the writer of Hebrews was not concerned with this aspect of Moses here. He left Moses' faithfulness unquestioned.

In Hebrews 3:3, the writer moved to a contrast to magnify the unmatched superiority of Jesus Christ. He extended this magnification of Jesus' superior status in two directions. Initially the writer presented an architectural analogy in verses 3-4, probably inspired by the reference to God's house in verse 2. In ancient times, the builder commonly received more acclaim than the building. As part of the house that Jesus built, Moses was less notable than the builder Himself. Moses was part of the creation, not the Creator. Secondly, Jesus was worthy of more glory than Moses because of their earthly roles. Moses was faithful as a servant, while Jesus was faithful as the Son. Moses was a servant in God's house, while Jesus was the Son over God's house. So not only was Jesus a second Moses—He was a better Moses.

We prove ourselves genuine occupants of God's house (v. 6) if we do not follow after those under Moses' leadership who had unbelieving hearts. The writer of Hebrews maintained a focused contrast between the Mosaic covenant and Jesus as Founder of the new covenant.[4] The writer of Hebrews desired to inspire his readers to take appropriate action in response to the great examples of faithfulness presented to them, namely, Moses, but especially Jesus. While Moses was a good example, Jesus is the ultimate example. The writer's audience was not to follow the example of the grumbling mob of dissenting, faithless Israelites whose bodies were strewn in the desert.

> While Moses was a good example, Jesus is the ultimate example.

The theme of temptation is important in the comparison as Hebrews 2:18, the verse immediately preceding the key passage about Moses, tells us: "Because he himself suffered when he was tempted, he is able to help those who are being tempted" (Hebrews 2:18, NIV). When we examine Jesus' temptation account in Luke 4:1-13, we see that each of Jesus' scriptural responses to Satan's temptations is rooted in the "wilderness wandering" passages in Deuteronomy. Unlike the Israelites, Jesus, our great High Priest, "has been tempted in every way, just as we are— yet was without sin" (Heb. 4:15, NIV).[5]

Later, the writer of Hebrews gave Moses space in his hall of fame lineup in 11:23-29. He wanted to make sure his readers kept the proper focus: "Let us fix our eyes on Jesus, the author and perfecter of our faith" (12:2, NIV).

Adapted from "Moses in the Book of Hebrews" by Paul N. Jackson, Biblical Illustrator, fall 2006, 46–49. For further study, look for "Hebrews: The Nearness of King Jesus Biblical Illustrator Bundle" on lifeway.com/hebrews.

1. R. Kent Hughes, Hebrews, Preaching the Word, vol. 1 (Wheaton: Crossway Books, 1993), 89–91.
2. George H. Guthrie, "Hebrews" in Zondervan Illustrated Bible Background Commentary, Clinton E. Arnold, gen. ed., vol. 4 (Grand Rapids: Zondervan, 2002), 21–22.
3. George H. Guthrie, Hebrews in NIV Application Commentary (Grand Rapids: Zondervan,1998).
4. William L. Lane, Hebrews 1–8, Word Biblical Commentary, vol. 47A (Dallas: Word Books, 1991), 73. Hebrews refers to Moses again in 7:14; 8:5; 9:19; 10:28; 11:24; and 12:21.
5. Jesus quoted Deuteronomy 8:3; 6:13; and 6:16.

"Let us go on to maturity" in Greek is pheromai, *which means* _____ ____ ____ _____ ____ .

The word _____ *in Hebrew actually means* _____ .

What was in the ark of the covenant?

1.

2.

3.

The curtain ripped from ____ *to bottom. It implies that* ____ _____ *did the rending.*

Discussion Questions:

1. *How has Jesus carried you through the challenges and difficulties in life toward spiritual maturity?*

2. *Why is it sometimes difficult for us to receive criticism and warnings that would help us mature as believers?*

3. *What steps will you take this week to "grow up" and move toward maturity in your faith?*

Video sessions available for purchase
at www.lifeway.com/hebrews

WHY ALL THE DRAMA ABOUT A MAN NAMED MEL?

WALK A MILE IN HEBREW SHOES

Last weekend my dear friends Ginny Bishop Lyden and Brenda Brown Nell—the same two with whom I pranced around the front yard, pretending to be gymnasts—came to Nashville for a long-overdue reunion. We spent the better part of 36 hours belly-laughing as we reminisced about our antics in high school. Ginny, who still has the body of a supermodel, the mind of a nuclear physicist, and the memory of an elephant (the only reason I'm not tempted to tape a Kick Me sign to her back is that her beauty and brilliance are eclipsed by her kindness), regaled us with stories about our adolescent antics that I'd forgotten.

Like the time she, Tracie Reynolds, and I dressed up in giant, tacky, Three Little Pig ensembles and careened down the sloped aisles of our high school auditorium on Rollerblades in front of our classmates in an attempt to increase school spirit and yearbook sales. Ginny had to remind me of the details of our pig-tastrophe. Tracie, who was not very agile to begin with and therefore quite clumsy while zooming downhill in a swine costume on skates, shrieked and flailed before crashing into the stage with a wood-splintering *THWAK!* causing Ginny and I to double over with guffaws and wet our pants/pig costumes. I probably suppressed that memory on purpose.

What's the craziest outfit you've ever worn to make a point or highlight a theme (say, dressing up as a cartoon character for your child's birthday party)?

Who's your favorite advertising character (the Geico gecko, the Energizer Bunny, that cute Chihuahua from Taco Bell, etc.)?

Once I dressed up as a character from the soap opera *Dallas* (complete with sassy red cowboy boots, big hair, and a fake gun) and reenacted a scene from the "Who Shot J.R.?" episode for the talent portion of the Miss Seminole High School pageant. Suffice it to say, my embarrassing will-someone-please-dig-a-hole-fast-so-I-can-disappear-into-it attempt at "talent" ruined any chance I had of winning the pageant, and I haven't worn heels with a bathing suit since.

Oh and who could forget the time we dressed up in gaudy ball gowns and lip-synced "Ain't No Mountain High Enough"—courtesy of a Diana Ross and the Supremes cassette tape—in front of the whole school. Or the time we sought to increase participation in the student council election. We looped around the parking lot on scooters with mega-phones and sandwich boards, encouraging people to "Scoot On In and Vote." It's a good thing we had tight skin and high metabolisms back then, because, boy, did we have a cheesy habit of using props to get our point across.

Which brings me to this mysterious man named Melchizedek *(mel-kiz-eh-deck)* who takes up an entire chapter in the Book of Hebrews. So what's the big deal about this dude with the weird name (which I sometimes shorten to "Mel" for pronunciation's sake)? Well, the bottom line is that Melchizedek is not unlike our pig ensembles, my towering *Dallas* coiffure, or the scooters we commandeered for voter awareness: he's essentially a prop—a tangible tool the pastor of Hebrews used to illustrate some critical concepts to his baby-Christian congregation.

LEAN INTO THE STORY

Before we attempt to mine the jewels from Melchizedek's story, let's take a short detour to consider the concept of religious comfort zones. You know—the places, things, or routines that become like spiritual La-Z-Boys. We settle so deeply into them that (before you know it) we've made an indentation shaped like our rear ends, and we find ourselves stuck in a rut that's hard to escape. We take people, activities, and objects God has used to communicate His grace to one generation and turn them into objects of idol worship.

What other good things might we be making part of our "religious rut"—or worse, turning into false idols?

For a biblical example, consider Numbers 21. The people had spoken against God and against Moses. As punishment, God sent poisonous snakes among them. In Numbers 21:9, God instructed Moses to make a bronze snake and place it on a pole. The people who had been bitten by the deadly snakes could look to the bronze snake on the pole and be healed. Properly understood at the time, the bronze snake was a great teaching aid about trusting God—a pictorial reminder of His faithfulness. The far greater purpose of the bronze snake became clear later in God's revelation. It foreshadowed the Savior and the cross. Jesus clearly applied the Numbers episode to Himself:

"Just as Moses lifted up the snake in the wilderness,
so the Son of Man must be lifted up."

JOHN 3:14 (HCSB)

In what sense is Jesus' presence on the cross like the bronze snake on the pole in Moses' day?

So far, so good. But, from Moses' time, move forward in Israel's history a few hundred years to 2 Kings 18, when Isaiah was God's prophet and Hezekiah was king. The people had become extremely rebellious. They worshiped false gods at "high places" all over the land. Hezekiah instituted reforms, including tearing down the altars to the false gods. Now look at verse 4:

> He [Hezekiah] removed the high places, shattered the sacred pillars, and cut down the Asherah poles. He broke into pieces the bronze snake that Moses made, for the Israelites burned incense to it up to that time.
>
> 2 KINGS 18:4 (HCSB)

The people had taken a sacred object and turned it into an obscenity. They made something that pictured their coming Savior into an object used in the worship of false gods.

Moses' story offers another example of the same principle. When the time came for him to die, God did something unprecedented in Scripture. He buried Moses and kept his grave site secret (Deut. 34:5-6).

Judging from what the people did with the bronze snake, why do you think God may have kept Moses' body out of their hands?

An additional clue appears in the New Testament. Jude 1:9 says that Michael the archangel, "was disputing with the Devil in a debate about Moses' body" (HCSB). Both the episodes with Moses' snake and his body may point to the same thing. We take the thing God used to communicate His grace and make it into a spiritual La-Z-Boy. Our ability to make an idol from something good seems limitless.

Do you resonate more with a formal worship environment (dress clothes and hymns) or a more informal church environment (blue jeans and guitars)? Why do you feel more comfortable worshipping in that particular environment?

Which translation of the Bible do you prefer and why?

What new trends in Christian culture make you uncomfortable?

Which ones do you enjoy?

What ancient traditions of Christian culture do you hope the community of faith continues to observe?

Just as we are attached to our preferences, the Hebrews had a Velcro-like attachment to the priesthood. Established at the beginning of their history as a theocracy, the priesthood formed the backbone of their position as God's chosen people. Not too long after a bottle was broken on the bow of Judaism, God Himself proclaimed both the need for and the order of the Levitical priesthood. Therefore, the priesthood had become part of their national identity, as important to the Jews as their Abrahamic heritage and the promised land they inherited after four centuries of captivity in Egypt and four decades of wandering in the wilderness.

So you can imagine how difficult the idea of a new High Priest was for them, particularly one who made the Levitical priesthood they were so fond of and familiar with obsolete. Which brings us to the need for a really good preaching prop.

We're about to encounter some challenging concepts, so let's break the unfamiliar (to us, not to the original hearers) passage into more understandable bites. As we go through chapter 7, make notes while I give you some directions with each portion. Please take the time to do each activity. I promise the message will be clearer that way.

Go through Hebrews 7:1-3 carefully, word by word and phrase by phrase. Beside each element of the pastor's case, write items that sound as though they might apply to Jesus. Read Genesis 14:17-20 and Psalm 110:1-4.

¹For this Melchizedek—

King of Salem, priest of the Most High God,

who met Abraham and blessed him

as he returned from defeating the kings,

²and Abraham gave him a tenth of everything;

first, his name means king of righteousness,

then also, king of Salem,

meaning king of peace;

³without father, mother, or genealogy,

having neither beginning of days nor end of life,

but resembling the Son of God—

remains a priest forever.

HEBREWS 7:1-3 (HCSB)

Who was Melchizedek?

Did you notice the words in verse 3, "having neither beginning of days nor end of life"? The NCV paraphrases the passage, "No one knows ... when he was born, or when he died." That translation of the phrase suggests they chose the first of two opinions scholars hold about Melchizedek.

1. Some believe Melchizedek was a human character in Genesis. As a human, he would have died, but we're just not told about his death. Therefore, the pastor uses him as a prop to prove his argument.

2. Others hold that Melchizedek was a supernatural, preincarnate appearance of Jesus—a christophany. Therefore, the pastor uses him as a prop to prove his argument.

Solid, Bible-believing scholars hold to each opinion. Note that Psalm 110 definitely puts Melchizedek in a Messianic context either way. You can read the passages and decide for yourself. Or, like me, you can leave the question open and marvel at the fact that God wrote Melchizedek into Genesis 14 and Psalm 110 many centuries before the pastor would need Melchizedek to make the truth about Jesus clear. Just don't miss the remarkable air of mystery God wrapped around this priest of Salem. What a mighty God, who can span two millennia from Abraham to Jesus, all to lift up His Son.

Melchizedek was a great prop to illustrate the difference between the perfect priesthood of Jesus Christ and the Levitical priesthood for several reasons. First, his title is the "king of Salem," and the word "Salem" comes from the same Hebrew root as the word *shalom* or "peace."[1] Therefore, it's not too much of a stretch to call Melchizedek the "king of peace," which sounds a lot like the Prince of peace title Isaiah ascribed to Immanuel (Isaiah 9:6). Did you note that while reading through the passage?

Melchizedek's also an effective metaphor for the Messiah because no one knows who his father or mother was (verse 3), so he basically came from nowhere. Jesus was born of a virgin, so that makes His genealogy unique too.

If you were on a let's-ascribe-a-new-title-for-King-Jesus committee, what title would you give Him that hasn't been used before?

If you were to spend the afternoon with Mary, the mother of Jesus, what would you do and what would you ask her?

Then there's the whole Melchizedek-wasn't-a-Levite-but-Abraham-still-put-a-check-in-Melchizedek's-offering-plate thing.

Read the next portion of Hebrews, marking the elements of the pastor's argument that Jesus' priesthood is greater than the Levitical priesthood. Plan to write your summary of the argument following the passage. Remember, the pastor's premise is Melchizedek > Levi; therefore, Jesus' priesthood > the Levitical priesthood.

You can see how great Melchizedek was. Abraham, the great father, gave him a tenth of everything that he won in battle. Now the law says that those in the tribe of Levi who become priests must collect a tenth from the people—their own people—even though the priests and the people are from the family of Abraham. Melchizedek was not from the tribe of Levi, but he collected a tenth from Abraham. And he blessed Abraham, the man who had God's promises. Now everyone knows that the more important person blesses the less important person. Priests receive a tenth, even though they are only men who live and then die. But Melchizedek, who received a tenth from Abraham, continues living, as the Scripture says. We might even say that Levi, who receives a tenth, also paid it when Abraham paid Melchizedek a tenth. Levi was not yet born, but he was in the body of his ancestor when Melchizedek met Abraham. The people were given the law concerning the system of priests from the tribe of Levi, but they could not be made perfect through that system. So there was a need for another priest to come, a priest like Melchizedek, not Aaron. And when a different kind of priest comes, the law must be changed, too. We are saying these things about Christ, who belonged to a different tribe. No one from that tribe ever served as a priest at the altar. It is clear that our Lord came from the tribe of Judah, and Moses said nothing about priests belonging to that tribe.

HEBREWS 7:4-14 (NCV)

List as many elements of the pastor's argument for the superiority of Melchizedek's (and, therefore, Jesus') priesthood as you could spot in the passage:

The fact that Melchizedek did not descend from Levi was a huge, hairy deal to the Hebrews. Much like you have to have valid identification to get into the gate area of an airport nowadays, a Jewish man had to have Levitical lineage to get into the priesthood. Which is why the Hebrews' pastor goes to such great lengths to prove that being a Levite wasn't a nonnegotiable qualification for the priesthood like they'd always been taught.

God's stamp of approval totally trumped being born into the "right family." These young Jewish believers simply had to wrap their minds around this foreign concept; otherwise, the priesthood of Jesus (who came from the tribe of Judah rather than the priestly tribe of Levi) would seem illegitimate to them. So their spiritual leader whips the ace out of his sleeve and explains that Abraham, the beloved patriarch of the entire Jewish race, paid a tithe to Melchizedek, proving beyond a shadow of a doubt that he was indeed a priest even though he didn't have one drop of Levitical blood in his body.

You could have stated the passage's arguments in many different ways. Here are my summary statements showing that Jesus' priesthood is greater than the Levitical priesthood.

- Abraham tithed to Melchizedek long before Levi was born, and since Levi was "in" Abraham (genetically), Levi paid tithes to Melchizedek. Hence Melchizedek is greater than Levi.

- Melchizedek blessed Abraham, and only the greater can bless the lesser.

- Human priests all die; Melchizedek didn't.

- Levi's priesthood couldn't perfect anybody; Jesus' does.

   Read Genesis 14:17-24 and Leviticus 27:30-33. Since the first mention of tithing occurs after Abraham's encounter with Melchizedek in the Old Testament, what do you think prompted Abraham to pay homage to Melchizedek?

What prompts you to tithe?

On a scale of 1 to 10, with 1 being "I spend more at Starbucks than I tithe at church" and 10 being "I totally get what the Bible means when it talks about giving to God joyfully because I find myself grinning every time I put money in the offering plate," where would you honestly place yourself in this season?

1————————————————————————————————10
Starbucks Bucks   *Joyful Giver*

Finally, there's the whole timeless-reign thing Jesus and Melchizedek had in common.

> And this becomes even more clear when we see that another priest comes who is like Melchizedek. He was not made a priest by human rules and laws but through the power of his life, which continues forever. It is said about him, "You are a priest forever, a priest like Melchizedek."

HEBREWS 7:15-17 (NCV)

In Hebrews the pastor constantly quoted the Old Testament. In verse 17 he quoted Psalm 110:4. My question seems too obvious, but humor me. Why is an endless life essential to an effective priesthood?

The old rule is now set aside, because it was weak and useless. The Law of Moses could not make anything perfect. But now a better hope has been given to us, and with this hope, we can come near to God. That God did this with an oath is important. Others became priests without an oath, but Christ became a priest with God's oath. God said:

> "The LORD has made a promise and will not change his mind. He said, 'You are a priest forever.'"

PSALM 110:4 (NCV)

In the final portion of chapter 7, circle the statements sealing the pastor's argument that Jesus' priesthood is the best.

This means that Jesus is the guarantee of a better agreement from God to his people. When one of the other priests died, he could not continue being a priest. So there were many priests. But because Jesus lives forever, he will never stop serving as priest. So he is able always to save those who come to God through him because he always lives, asking God to help them. Jesus is the kind of high priest we need. He is holy, sinless, pure, not influenced by sinners, and he is raised above the heavens. He is not like the other priests who had to offer sacrifices every day, first for their own sins, and then for the sins of the people. Christ offered his sacrifice only once and for all time when he offered himself. The law chooses high priests who are people with weaknesses, but the word of God's oath came later than the law. It made God's Son to be the high priest, and that Son has been made perfect forever.

HEBREWS 7:22-28 (NCV)

One of the last requests my dad, Harper, made before he passed away was to help him change into a pair of clean pajamas, his nice robe, and his good slippers. When the hospice nurse asked him why (because completely changing his clothes was going to be quite an ordeal and physically painful for him), Dad furrowed his brows and said in his typically gruff voice, "Because I'm about to be dancing on streets of gold and I don't want to show up barefoot and half-dressed!"

My father knew that heaven was going to be a glorious celebration that lasted forever, as opposed to the bumpy and often sad road he'd journeyed down for eighty years on this side of glory. Which is why he was so determined to wear a nice outfit when it was his turn for a timeless waltz with the angels.

The pastor of Hebrews is trying to teach his friends what my daddy already believed: that our Creator-Redeemer loves His children so much, He provides only the best for us. Jesus is not a "mostly effective" priest who offers "pretty good" sacrifices. He doesn't "almost always" remember our needs when He intercedes with God the Father on our behalf. He always has compassion for sinners like us. He completely covered the debt mankind owed God for our depravity. He is our perfect High Priest, without fault or blemish. And that, ladies and gentleman, will never, not ever, no never change.

Which of Christ's Melchizedek-like traits do you appreciate the most: his abnormal genealogy, his lack of Levitical blood, or his timeless reign? Why?

How would you describe the "forever" aspect of Christ's reign to a child?

Read Romans 8:34. In light of the way this verse depicts Jesus interceding for us with our Heavenly Father, what do you think He's been talking to God about lately with regards to you?

SCOOT YOUR CHAIR A LITTLE CLOSER TO JESUS

When I was eight years old, my dad surprised me by buying the most beautiful horse I'd ever seen. Her name was Gypsy and she was a roan-colored quarter horse with a long black mane and tail, one white sock on her left front hoof, and a not-yet-tame disposition. Every Friday afternoon for two years, on the way to his house from Mom's (my parents divorced when I was five and I spent most weekends with my father), I begged Dad to drive by the pasture she pranced in, which belonged to a friend of his. He usually sighed and gave in, then waited impatiently while I coaxed a typically snorting, rearing Gypsy to the fence with apples or sugar cubes. Of course, I never thought I'd be lucky enough to call that magnificent beast my own. That'd be like buying a tornado or a tidal wave. It was enough to just gaze at her while she galloped triumphantly across a field, nostrils flaring and tail flying high like a banner.

Then one day while I was in a happy daze, leaning against the fence and watching Gypsy, Dad said something along the lines of, "So, do you think you could get a bridle on that horse?" I told him I wasn't sure, but I'd be willing to try. "Good," he replied, "because I just bought her for you. Now help me get this trailer hooked up so we can load her up."

I was so stunned, you could've knocked me over with a feather. I don't remember much else about that particular Friday afternoon, except that after we got Gypsy situated in the horse-trailer, I asked Dad if I could ride in the back of the truck instead of in the cab with him, because I couldn't bear to look away from her. And from that moment on for the next six years, every Friday afternoon until Sunday when Dad drove me back to Mom's, that four-legged bucking bullet and I were inseparable.

Gypsy was way more than just a mode of transportation to me; she was my trusted confidant through the sometimes-turbulent years of adolescence. She would shift sideways and gently push against me when I opened the door to her stall—almost as if she knew a people-pleasing middle child who was shuttled back and forth between two homes needed something sturdy to lean on. Plus, Gypsy was loyal. She refused to budge, stubbornly stomping her hooves and shaking her big head if anyone other than Dad or me attempted to ride her. Finally, she gave me confidence. Since Dad's ranch was in a rural area, forty miles away from Mom's, I didn't know any of the kids in his neighborhood when we moved there. And since I was not only the new girl but a city girl to boot, I wasn't sure I'd fit in. However, one of the first social outings we were invited to involved a horse race and Gypsy's lightening-fast speed earned me immediate acceptance into our town's Future Farmers of America clique.

Interestingly enough, when a friend invited me to go on a trail ride with her a few years ago, I hated it. My steed was nice, albeit older than Methuselah, and the scenery was beautiful. But the nose-to-tail monotony of poking along on a docile "rented" horse simply couldn't compare to racing the wind with Gypsy. Even though it's been decades since she and I left farm boys in our dust, she's the horse my heart remembers. I just couldn't get comfortable with another ride. So when I got home, I revved up all 650 horses in my Yamaha V Star Classic motorcycle and went for a different kind of ride as a tribute to the greatest horse I've ever known.

Does anything in your relationship to Jesus resonate with my story of Gypsy? If so, please tell me about it.

How do you think the persecuted Jewish believers may have felt about trusting someone new and unfamiliar?

When I began studying Hebrews and tried to imagine what it was like for them to accept the priesthood of Jesus after centuries of familiarity with the Levitical priesthood, I couldn't help but think of how awkward I felt on that trail ride with a strange horse lumbering along underneath me. Although the "poky" and "docile" parts of that equine ride certainly don't apply to our Savior, the "new" and "different" parts do. And human nature tends to be highly resistant to anything other than the familiar.

The term "highly resistant" is a mild description of how first-century Jews reacted to the idea of an incarnate Messiah who perfectly fulfilled every jot and tittle of Mosaic Law and established a new order based on relationship with God instead of legalistic adherence to religious rules. In fact, the Book of Acts explains that the accusation Jewish scribes and elders brought against Stephen and then stoned him for was this: "This man never ceases to speak words against this holy place and the law, for we have heard him say that this Jesus of Nazareth will destroy this place and will change the customs that Moses delivered to us" (Acts 6:13b-14).

Concerns about how following Jesus could alter their way of life whipped these Jewish dudes in Acts—some of whom were undoubtedly related to the recipients of our letter—into a murderous frenzy.

So you can see why the pastor of Hebrews resorts to using colorful, somewhat brow-raising props like Melchizedek to help emphasize the "better than" aspect of Christ's ministry. He was basically facing a firewall of resistance with nothing more than a bucket of living water. Dousing his friends with the truth over and over again was necessary for them to be awash in a brand new way of interacting with Yahweh.

What family traditions are important to you (e.g., eating the same meal at the same time every Thanksgiving, followed by a nap and then a game of touch football)?

How do you think you'd respond to someone changing the family traditions you hold most dear, especially if they didn't consult you first?

LIVE THE STORY OUT LOUD

1. *At least one day this week, part your hair on the opposite side from your normal part or fix it in a completely new way. Make a mental note of whether it feels weird to wear a different hairstyle.*

2. *If your study is a large group that usually breaks up into smaller groups, ask another small group to switch tables or locations with you this week. On a scale of 1 ("no biggie") to 10 ("very frustrating"), how did it affect you to move from where you normally meet to a new setting?*

3. *The next time you attend worship at your church, sit somewhere you've never sat before (if you normally sit near the back, sit up front; if you've never sat in the balcony, go up there). Ask yourself (and your family if you attend church with them) how it felt to move from the seat/pew you're familiar with. Was it a mostly pleasant experience, engaging in worship from a different viewpoint? Or did sitting in a new area distract you from fully engaging in worship?*

4. *Ask the oldest member of your family what his/her favorite character traits and traditions are from your ancestors. Which would you like to emulate? Which are you proud of?*

5. *Try to find an old family Bible (if your parents are still living, ask to borrow one of theirs) and scan the pages to see what notes have been written in the margins.*

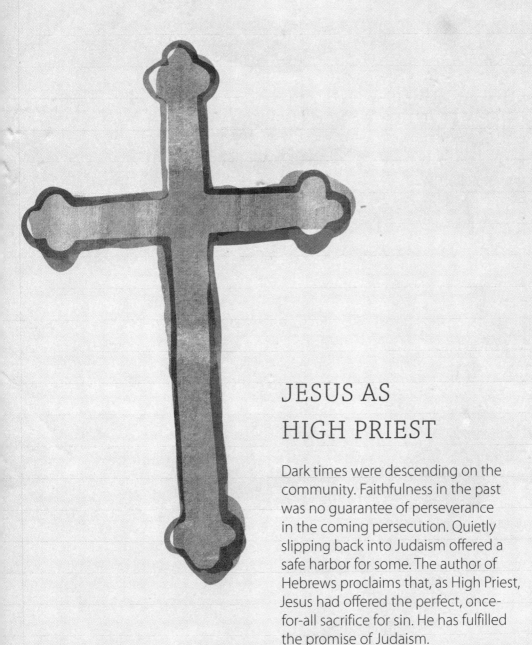

JESUS AS HIGH PRIEST

Dark times were descending on the community. Faithfulness in the past was no guarantee of perseverance in the coming persecution. Quietly slipping back into Judaism offered a safe harbor for some. The author of Hebrews proclaims that, as High Priest, Jesus had offered the perfect, once-for-all sacrifice for sin. He has fulfilled the promise of Judaism.

The author's audience were no strangers to sacrifice and priesthood. But when he picked an image and time frame to picture for his readers, he didn't turn to the temple and the priests of his own day. He returned to the time of the exodus and the tabernacle.[1] The history of the Jewish priesthood may explain why and provide a background for understanding the author's christology of Jesus as High Priest.

> The high priests were influential; and the office was seen by most Jews as a holy office.

God designated the tribe of Levi as special representatives of the people in religious matters. Of the tribe of Levi, Aaron and his sons were set apart as priests to mediate God's covenant with Israel and maintain the purity of the nation.[2] As chief priest (Lev. 21:10), Aaron wore the priestly vestments. On the Day of Atonement he alone could enter the Holy of Holies to offer sacrifices for the sins of the people. At Aaron's death, his son Eleazar assumed the high priest's role.

During Israel's early history, sacrifices were performed in the enclosed tabernacle/temple by priests but apparently could be performed on open-air altars by any Jewish male.[3] For example, Gideon and Elijah offered sacrifices (Judg. 6:1-26; 1 Kings 18), and the sons of David were called priests, presumably in connection with the private sacrifices of the king (2 Sam. 8:18).[4] When David established the monarchy, leadership was shared by representatives of both Eleazar and Aaron's other son, Ithamar. However, by the time of Solomon, Eleazar's descendant Zadok was established as the high priest. Throughout the monarchy and into the postexilic period, descendants of Zadok continued to serve as high priest. Descendants of Aaron's other son served as priests but were not considered eligible to serve as high priest.

During the inter-biblical period, bribery became the means to attain the high priesthood. Jason won the office of high priest from his brother Onias by bribing Antiochus IV (175 B.C.). Several years later Menelaus, a non-Zadokite, outbid Jason and was appointed high priest by Antiochus. After the Jewish rebellion by the Maccabees, Jonathan, one of the Maccabees brothers, took over the position of high priest. The descendants of the leaders of the rebellion continued to serve as high priests. With the advent of the Romans and Herod the Great, bribery was once again the primary method of acquiring the office of the high priest. From 37 B.C. until A.D. 67, Herod or the Romans appointed and deposed 28 different high priests, 25 of whom came from non-legitimate families.[5] In spite of the loss of status caused by frequent changes, the high priests were influential; and the office was seen by most Jews as a holy office.[6]

Against this background the author of Hebrews set forth Jesus as the perfect High Priest. The theme of the priesthood appeared in the prologue to the book even though the designation "high priest" is not used. Jesus is the One who made purification for sins (Heb. 1:3), a distinctly high-priestly function.

At the end of the first section the author introduced the high priest theme explicitly: Jesus is a merciful and faithful High Priest in God's service (Heb. 2:17). The author first expanded on the faithfulness of Jesus by comparing Him to Moses (Heb. 3:1-6), followed by a warning about the necessity of remaining faithful (Heb. 3:7–4:14). The warning ends with a challenge to "hold fast the confession" since we have such a great High Priest as Jesus (Heb 4:14).[7] The rest of the second major section develops the thought of Jesus as merciful High Priest (4:15–5:10). In 2:17-18, the author listed two functions that Jesus fulfilled in this role: He atoned for the sins of the people, and He was able to help

> As the merciful High Priest, Jesus atoned for the sins of the people and was able to help the ones being tested.

the ones being tested. These two functions appear again in 5:1. A high priest must offer gifts and sacrifices for sins, and he must deal gently with the ignorant and those who have gone astray. Jesus is the superior High Priest. The high priests of the Jerusalem temple had to offer a sacrifice for their own sins (5:3). Jesus had no need to offer sacrifices on His own behalf. He was without sin, (4:15) yet He identified fully with sinners.

One did not enter the Jerusalem priesthood by choice. Though foreign rulers often tried to thwart God's plan, He had designated Aaron and his sons to serve Him as priests. Since Jesus' lineage was traced through David, an explanation was needed as to how Jesus could function as High Priest. That explanation was found by referring to Melchizedek, an obscure Old Testament figure mentioned only in Genesis 14:17-24 and Psalm 110:4. The development of the explanation was delayed until the third major section of the letter, but the author insisted that God had designated Jesus as High Priest according to the order of Melchizedek (5:10). As High Priest Jesus became the "source of eternal salvation to everyone who obeyed him" (v. 9).

The third major section (5:11–10:39) is the longest section in Hebrews, bracketed by two of the most severe warning passages in the book (5:11–6:20 and 10:19-39). These two warning passages are similar in form;

and though they are severe, both end on a positive note of encouragement. Both also mention Jesus as High Priest passing through the curtain, an obvious reference to the Day of Atonement ritual when the high priest entered the holy of holies.

> Melchizedek's lack of lineage allowed the author to compare him to Jesus.

In this third major section the author systematically developed how Jesus surpassed the Old Testament priesthood. First, the author explained the implications of the relationship between Jesus' priesthood and Melchizedek's (chap. 7). Unlike Aaron's lineage, which could be traced, Melchizedek's lack of lineage allowed the author to compare him to Jesus. Aaron died and was succeeded. Not so with Jesus, who remains a Priest forever. Since Abram gave tithes to Melchizedek (the lesser gives to the greater) and Melchizedek blessed Abram (the greater blesses the lesser), a priest after the order of Melchizedek must be superior to one like Aaron, a descendant of Abram.

In Psalm 110, the psalmist said the Lord swore that He would establish His chosen one as a Priest after the order of Melchizedek. The author of Hebrews picked up on this oath as a second sign of superiority. Aaron's descendants, though mediators of God's covenant with Israel, were established by the law. The oath of Psalm 110 was a sign of the new covenant of which Jesus was Mediator (Heb. 7:22).

The rest of this section up to the fourth warning passage is bracketed by references to Jeremiah's new covenant. In 8:8-12 the author quoted Jeremiah 31:31-34, and in 10:16-17 he quoted Jeremiah 31:33-34 again. This new covenant, which replaced the old covenant with Aaron as high priest, is superior in at least two ways. First the high priest of the old covenant was the only one who could enter the holy place; and he was limited to once a year. Access to God was effectively restricted for the people. Jesus entered the heavenly place and provided eternal salvation for those who obey Him (5:9), bold access to God (4:16), and eventually, salvation at His second coming (9:28).

The new covenant also surpasses the old in the nature of the sacrifice. The old covenant required the priests to carry the blood of animals into the holy place year after year for the sins of the people. The repetition of the sacrifices showed they could only remove ritual impurity. They did not affect the conscience. Jesus, carrying not an animal sacrifice but Himself, obtained eternal redemption (9:12) and purified our consciences (9:14). The author concluded by reminding his readers that the sacrificial system was no longer necessary: "Where there is forgiveness of these, there is no longer a sacrifice for sin" (10:18).

As High Priest of God's new covenant, Jesus provided for the readers everything that the old covenant could only suggest. As both High Priest and sacrifice, Jesus opened the way to God for all time. A return to Judaism was a return to the old, ineffective covenant that could only promise but not produce.

The fourth warning is based on this new freedom gained through Jesus' high priestly office (10:19-21), but the author dropped the image of Jesus as High Priest in the fourth major section of the book (11:1-12:13). Finally, the fifth section (12:14-13:25) reintroduces the priestly image and Day of Atonement language. Here, though, the author reminded his readers that all this discussion of high priest and sacrifice was not just theoretical jargon. In 13:10-13, he makes one more extension of the imagery. After the high priest offered the sacrifice, the carcass of the

> The author concluded by reminding his readers that the sacrificial system was no longer necessary.

sacrificial animal was burned outside the camp. As both High Priest and sacrifice, Jesus suffered outside the gate. The readers, for whom this sacrifice was made, must leave the safety of the city and move outside to suffer with the one who suffered for them.

Adapted from "Jesus as High Priest" by Charles A. Ray, Jr., Biblical Illustrator, summer 1997, 50–54. For further study, look for "Hebrews: The Nearness of King Jesus Biblical Illustrator Bundle" on lifeway.com/ hebrews.

1. *Neither of the two Greek words for temple commonly used in the New Testament,* hieron *and* naos, *are used in the Book of Hebrews. In their place the author used the word "tabernacle,"* skene, *10 times. All word searches were done using acCordance Ver. 1.1 (Vancouver, WA: The GRAMCORD Institute) .*
2. *Raymond Abba, "Priests and Levites" in* The Interpreter's Dictionary of the Bible, *vol. 3 (New York: Abingdon Press, 1962), 877–78.*
3. *Menahem Haran, "Priests and Priesthood" in* Encyclopaedia Judaica, *vol. 13, eds. Cecil Roth and Geoffrey Wigoder (Jerusalem: Keter Publishing House Ltd., 1971), 1072–73.*
4. *Ibid, 1072.*
5. *Jürgen Baehr, "Priest" in* The New International Dictionary of New Testament Theology, *vol. 3, ed. Colin Brown (Grand Rapids: Zondervan Publishing House, 1978), 35.*
6. *E. P. Sanders,* Judaism: Practice and Belief *(Philadelphia: Trinity Press International, 1992), 327.*
7. *All quotations from the New Testament are the writer's own translations based on the United Bible Society's Greek New Testament, fourth edition.*

Three Most Important Offices:

1. _____

2. _____

3. _____

Hebrews 8:6-7

Hebrews 8:13

Hebrews 9:11-14

Hebrews 9:24-27

Hebrews 10:5-10

Luke 5:1-11

Matthew 17:1-13

Matthew 26:69-75

John 21:15-19

Video sessions available for purchase
at www.lifeway.com/hebrews

Discussion Questions:

1. *How would you live differently if you remembered daily that Jesus' death on the cross paid the sacrifice for us "once and for all"?*

2. *How do you think we could better minister to those who are dealing with the "mistake chapters" in their story?*

_____

_____

_____

_____

_____

_____

_____

_____

_____

_____

_____

_____

_____

POINT YOUR HEART TOWARD JESUS AND GO!

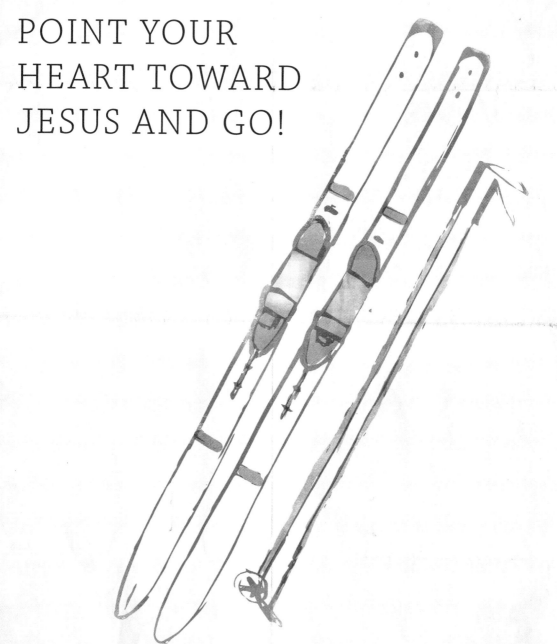

WALK A MILE IN HEBREW SHOES

One of my favorite activities in the whole world is snow-skiing. I just love the feeling of freedom that comes with flying down a steep slope on a cushion of white, sparkling powder. As a matter of fact, I've gotten "chapped throat" several times while skiing, because I can't help laughing out of sheer joy when I'm rocketing down a snow-covered hill on twin fiberglass sticks. However, the first time I stood in my skis on top of a Colorado mountain, I was much closer to crying than laughing. A few of my crazy friends (all ski instructors in college) decided that since I was a decent athlete with daredevil tendencies, we should skip the beginner slope and head straight to the double-black diamond, experts-only territory on the backside of Vail Mountain for my inaugural run.

I can still remember the fear surging through my mind and body as we glided (well, actually, they were the only ones gliding; I wobbled and lurched like a newborn calf) to the edge of the cliff they thought I'd have no problem skiing down. My friends started high-fiving each other and making jokes, giddy about our good fortune as the first skiers to venture into the back bowls of Vail that morning. Meanwhile, I stood there wide-eyed and mute, imagining myself cartwheeling out of control several thousand feet down until I splattered on the exposed rocks below. Not wanting to come across as a sissy-baby, I kept my apprehensions to myself, tried to herd my internal butterflies in the same general direction, and focused on not wetting my pants. (Especially since the Gortex pair I was squeezed into were borrowed, and the owner probably wouldn't appreciate such a tangible token of my terror.)

What's the scariest adventure you've been on recently?

How do you usually respond when you're in over your head? Do you clam up when you're apprehensive or do you advertise your panic?

With whoops of glee, four of my five so-called friends leapt off the cliff, executing perfect jump turns in the powdery snow—*WHOOSH, WHOOSH, WHOOSH*—down the almost vertical slope until they were wee neon dots below. Judy (who, in spite of being on the goading committee that ushered me to the mountaintop, remains my dearest friend) and I were the only ones left. She then clearly and calmly gave me some tips:

- Keep your shoulders square, facing the bottom of the hill (pretend like you have a headlight in each shoulder that has to be aimed straight ahead to "light the trail").

- When making a turn, swivel your hips, but keep the rest of your body—especially your shoulders—positioned toward the bottom of the hill.

- To make a left turn, put your weight on the outside edge of your left ski and press down on the little toe of that foot, as well as the big toe of right foot; to make a right turn, put your weight on the outside edge of your right ski and press down on the little toe of that foot, as well as the big toe of your left foot.

- The steeper the hill, the more turns you should make to keep your speed in check, so link your turns like continuous S's (since the double-black diamond run we were skiing down was super steep).

Then she smiled as if she'd just explained the easiest task in the world instead of directions on hurtling through space. I couldn't decide whether to smile back or punch her in the nose. What in the heck was an "edge"? How exactly did one "swivel" her hips (since as a Christian single woman, that wasn't an extracurricular activity I was familiar with)? How was I supposed to distinguish between my big toes and little toes while flailing down a mountainside, especially since all ten were frozen stubs at that point? And why in the world was she grinning in the face of impending doom? Perhaps the shock and confusion were evident in my open mouth and arched eyebrows, because Judy chuckled. Then she took hold of my elbow, helped me shuffle to the edge of the precipice, and said, "Just point your skis toward the bottom and go!"

So I did. And it was a total blast! Mind you, I rolled more than I stayed upright for the first two or three hundred yards, but the snow provided a soft cushion for crash landings, and by the time we got to the bottom, I couldn't wait to go back up and do it all over again. And I've been an avid skier ever since, although I still haven't mastered the whole headlight-pinky-toe-swiveling part.

After nine and a half chapters of establishing the theological foundation to support the superiority of King Jesus, the pastor of Hebrews decides it's time for his congregation to start practicing what he's been preaching. So he herds his sheep to the precipice of the radical-Christian-living hill and says, "Now point your heart toward Jesus and go!"

What is your greatest hesitancy when it comes to "jumping off the cliff" into a more radical Christian life? What do you fear losing if you jump?

What have your spiritual leaders done or said lately that encouraged you to commit to more radical Christian living?

LEAN INTO THE STORY

Just as Judy gave me tips on skiing downhill, the Hebrews' spiritual leader gives them some sage advice for navigating closer to Jesus:

Tip #1: Move toward Jesus with Confidence

> Therefore, brothers, since we have boldness to enter the sanctuary through the blood of Jesus, by a new and living way He has opened for us through the curtain (that is, His flesh), and since we have a great high priest over the house of God, let us draw near with a true heart in full assurance of faith, our hearts sprinkled clean from an evil conscience and our bodies washed in pure water.

HEBREWS 10:19-22 (HCSB)

Before we unpack this tip and zoom off the cliff toward committed Christian living, let's peruse three simple words in the above passage—"brothers" and "let us"—because they pack an emotional wallop. First of all, by using the term "brothers," the pastor of Hebrews again claims this motley crew of wobbly new believers as family. Instead of condemning them for their fear of being barbecued by one of Nero's cronies, he claims them as kin.

Then he goes a step further by using the first-person plural, "let *us* draw near," in his charge to move toward Jesus with confidence. In other words, although he's obviously more mature spiritually than his congregation, he doesn't consider himself above them; instead, he humbly acknowledges that he needs to practice what he's preaching too.

My dear friend Sheila Walsh is near the top of my believers-I-respect-bunches list. She's got more knowledge and understanding about God's Word than I do. She's infinitely more patient with airport delays than I am (don't ask how I know this). And she's plumbed the depths of suffering in this life without doubting God's sovereign goodness. In short, she's miles ahead of me in the walk of faith. Yet every single time I confess something I'm struggling with, she's genuinely empathetic and typically describes a season in her life when she wrestled with the same thing. Through twenty years of friendship, Sheila has never looked down her nose at me even when my faith was noticeably threadbare. She's so convinced of her own need for Jesus, she can't help but have compassion for other potential prodigals. It's the mark of a great leader—being so preoccupied with God's grace that she doesn't have time to read her own press releases.

Based on 1 Timothy 1:15, what virtue do Paul and the pastor of Hebrews seem to have in common?

To what modern day spiritual leader(s) would you ascribe the same virtue and why?

In his classic book, *Mere Christianity,* C. S. Lewis wrote: "As long as you are proud you cannot know God. A proud man is always looking down on things and people: and, of course, as long as you are looking down, you cannot see something that is above you."

How would you explain the Lewis' quote to a child?

Now back to the bulk of Hebrews 10:19-22. The pastor of Hebrews encourages his friends to "enter the sanctuary" and "draw near"—in other words, to move toward Jesus—with "boldness" and "full assurance" because Jesus is the "great" High Priest who has established a "new way" for them to connect with their Creator-Redeemer.

The old way for an Israelite meant waiting all year for the Day of Atonement. So for 364 days, they stored all their sins in massive, mental garbage bags. Then, on the highest holy day in the Jewish calendar, they hauled all their trash to the temple and trusted a single human high priest to haul their heavy garbage—along with the rest of Israel's—into the holy of holies and ask God's forgiveness for an entire landfill of lust, greed, envy, bitterness, resentment, hatred, sexual immorality, selfishness, neglect, and using bad words in traffic.

It's hard to imagine the anxiety those Israelites must've felt in asking that one man on that one day to access enough divine mercy to cover up the stench of their millions of mistakes. Ritual would be hard-pressed to provide that kind of miraculous relief.

The old way became more real for me during my last trip to Israel a few years ago. Our small tour group was in Jerusalem for Yom Kippur—the Day of Atonement—which is what the Hebrews 10:19-22 passage refers to and Hebrews 9:7 literally describes: "but into the second only the high priest goes, and he but once a year, and not without taking blood, which he offers for himself and for the unintentional sins of the people."

We heard the long, plaintive blast from the shofar (a ram's horn), signaling the beginning of Yom Kippur, as the sun was setting behind the walls of the Old City of Jerusalem. All the buttons on our hotel elevator lit up afterward, because to press a button is considered "work" and therefore sinful on the Day of Atonement.

Partly because I'm a glass-is-half-full optimist but mostly because I knew Yom Kippur still represents the forgiveness of sins for observant Jews, I assumed we were all going to be swept up in one big, happy celebration. Perhaps singing U2's "Freedom" song in unison, while dancing joyful Middle Eastern jigs. But that wasn't the case at all. Instead we were pretty much quarantined to our rooms without access to food or transportation because most of the hotel staff was understandably off that day (there was no danger of starvation because American tourists always come armed with snacks). So we spent the better part of Yom Kippur sitting on our balcony, watching thousands of Jews trudge toward the Great Synagogue of Jerusalem on King George Street and solemnly greet each other with the phrase, "Gamar Hatima Tova."

When Abraham, our precious Jewish guide, came to pick us up at the hotel the next day, I asked him what "Gamar Hatima Tova" meant. He said that it's actually a greeting in the form of a question, translated, "Will you be inscribed with a good inscription?" Then he said, "Lisa, we don't believe in grace and mercy the way you do. We believe in God's justice. And we hope that by remembering all the ways we've transgressed His law over the past year, we'll receive justice instead of wrath." His answer is one of the saddest commentaries on the weakness of religious ritual I've ever heard—a living illustration of the old covenant's inability to cleanse the heart of a worshipper.

All too often Christians proclaim "Jesus is all we need" doctrine yet practice faulty "Jesus plus" faith. For example, we anxiously fill in all our Bible study blanks not because we long to know Jesus more intimately, but because we fear that if we miss an item on our spiritual to-do list, then God might be mad at us and put us in a government-subsidized apartment in glory instead of the mansion He promises.

What are some of the "plus" behaviors you've tried to add to the sufficiency of Christ (perhaps even subconsciously) in an attempt increase your chance of being "inscribed with a good inscription"?

Read 1 John 5:1-5,13-15. How would you describe the relationship between approaching God with confidence and following God in obedience?

When I'm with Missy in Haiti, she usually skips toward the orphanage pavilion at mealtime with her head held high and a huge grin spread across her face, urgently pulling me behind her. She's discovered that when she's with me—her new *blanca mama*—she doesn't get turned away from the table. Instead I will make sure her plastic plate is piled high with almost everything she points to. Rice (a generous spoonful), chicken (two drumsticks), bread (a whole slice), tomatoes and cucumbers (all she wants), and mango (unlimited slices!). Long gone are the days when my baby had to beg and even then only got to eat four or five times a week. Her little brown belly is no longer swollen from malnutrition. My daughter's heart is growing more confident that when she's with me, she will be taken care of.

How much more so is it with God and His kids! Our Heavenly Father is so eternally committed to caring for us that He sent His only begotten Son to establish a new way of coming to the table. Instead of trying to balance our hefty hopes on the slender shoulders of one flawed human priest, we get to place them on the infinitely broad back of the Prince of peace. Jesus accomplished our reconciliation with God forever through His death and resurrection. His sacrifice on the cross shredded the curtain that separated sinners from a holy God. His blood washed away the stain of sin and the stigma of shame. And we now have constant access to the banqueting table of divine grace because of King Jesus!

What point do you think the pastor of Hebrews was trying to make when he compared the temple curtain to the flesh of Jesus? See Hebrews 7:25 and reread Hebrews 10:19-22.

The temple curtain/veil served a dual purpose—it separated people from the holy of holies for 364 days a year and became the entry point for the high priest on Yom Kippur. Jesus serves a similar dual purpose.

How would you explain that Jesus serves as the entry point to a relationship with God?

In what sense does Jesus serve to "separate" people from God?

If you had difficulty with that last question, you might consult John 3:18. Jesus offers "such a great salvation" (Heb. 2:3) to those who receive Him but warned us against neglecting that salvation. No person will ever be condemned for her sin. She will be condemned ultimately because she has refused Jesus' death for her sin. If we believe God's Word, we are stuck with the reality that many will spend eternity in hell. But they will have crawled over the sacrifice of Jesus to get there.

What divine sustenance do you need piled the highest on your proverbial plate this season: forgiveness, renewed hope, emotional/physical healing, or more faith in God's sovereign goodness?

All the chatter about snow skiing at the beginning of this section got me thinking about the first time I learned to water-ski. I was about thirteen when my Dad Angel traded in his bass boat for a ski boat and taught us how to slice across the surface of water on narrow boards at 30-35 miles an hour. One would think a feat like that would take a long time to learn, but my sister Theresa and I learned to water-ski pretty well in just one weekend because Dad insisted that we learn in his favorite liquid hangout—the St. Johns River: a really gorgeous Floridian waterway—if you don't mind the alligators.

Dad told us not to worry about all the floating "logs" that morphed into bumpy-backed monsters with big teeth. Yet we did notice them with growing horror as we motored to the stretch of river he decided was the perfect spot for beginning skiers. And he used the same phrase cavemen probably used to coax their kids outside when there was a T. rex in the yard: "Now, y'all don't worry. They're more afraid of you than you are of them." Yeah, right. And real grizzlies are jovial toilet-paper connoisseurs like in the Charmin commercial.

Needless to say, after Dad gently shoved our orange-vest-wearing selves over the side of the boat into the brackish brown water of the St. Johns, Theresa and I hung onto the ski rope as if our very lives depended on not letting go. Even after accidentally losing a ski when I careened across the wake, I wasn't about to let go of the handle. Because if I did, there was a good chance I'd become gator kibble, and I've never been a big fan of being chewed on.

Just like my sister and I learned to hold on, so the congregation of the Hebrews' pastor has been counseled to *hold on*, having been told three times already in this sermon:

1. Hebrews 3:6: Christ is faithful over God's house as a son. And we are his house if indeed we hold fast our confidence and our boasting in our hope.

2. Hebrews 3:14: For we have come to share in Christ, if indeed we hold our original confidence firm to the end.

3. Hebrews 4:14: Since then we have a great high priest who has passed through the heavens, Jesus, the Son of God, let us hold fast our confession.

Now the pastor ups the ante by adding the clause "without wavering" (Heb. 10:23). In other words, don't just hold on, but hold on and Don't. Let. Go. No. Matter. What. Our enemy is an aggressive carnivore with big teeth, so our motivation to cling to our confession is to keep from being chewed up. However, we're holding on to hope not by the strength of our grip, but by the faithfulness of God.

Read 1 Peter 1:3. What proof do you have that your faith in Jesus is "living"? In other words, what are some "signs of life" that show your heart is beating for God?

John Calvin referred to a believer's hope as the "child" of our faith. In what ways can you picture your faith in Jesus as "parenting" your hope?

Read the following promises. In each Scripture, mark the area of God's faithfulness described. All the verses are in the HCSB translation.

1 Thessalonians 5:23-24: Now may the God of peace Himself sanctify you completely. And may your spirit, soul, and body be kept sound and blameless for the coming of our Lord Jesus Christ. He who calls you is faithful, who also will do it.

2 Thessalonians 3:3: But the Lord is faithful; He will strengthen and guard you from the evil one.

1 Peter 4:19: So those who suffer according to God's will should, while doing what is good, entrust themselves to a faithful Creator.

1 John 1:9: If we confess our sins, He is faithful and righteous to forgive us our sins and to cleanse us from all unrighteousness.

In which of the above ways do you need to experience His faithfulness the most in this season of your life?

Tip #3: Encourage Others and Engage in Christian Community

And let us be concerned about one another in order to promote love and good works, not staying away from our worship meetings, as some habitually do, but encouraging each other, and all the more as you see the day drawing near.

HEBREWS 10:24-25 (HCSB)

At a recent women's conference in Peoria, Illinois, all the other speakers had to leave early (because there aren't a lot of direct flights into petite Peoria), so Jen Hatmaker and I ended up doing double-duty the second half of the event, which left us both craving Indian food. Nothing quite restores happily exhausted, spicy-food-loving Bible teachers like copious amounts of flat bread and chicken tikka masala. So we Googled "Indian food in Peoria" (which sounds like a quirky independent film title), found a restaurant with a cute name, called a cab, and were soon shoveling huge forkfuls of rice and chicken smothered in curry sauce into our mouths like starving truckers at a roadside diner.

Quite some time later, after we'd consumed enough chicken tikka masala, saag paneer, and chicken vindaloo to feed a large family (Jen wasn't quite as piggish as I was), we clambered into another cab to go back to the hotel. At that point, I was in full Indian-food-coma posture—pupils dilated, top button of jeans undone, labored breathing, with a line of sweat above my lips from ingesting too much industrial-strength curry. It was all I could do not to beg Jen to ride on the hood so I could prostrate myself across the back-seat and groan in agony as the rice continued to swell in my already-stretched tummy.

Instead, I winced while situating my overstuffed self upright in the backseat, then asked our thirty-something, generously tattooed and pierced cabbie how he was doing. In all honesty, I didn't have an emotional investment in his well-being at that point; I really just wanted to get to my room as quickly as possible so I could be miserable in private. But greeting perfect strangers with a friendly "Hey, how ya doin'?" is second nature for Southerners, and it flew out of my mouth before I could snatch it back. But instead of responding with a noncommittal "Fine," he turned around to face us and said sincerely, "I'm not doing too well, but I'm sure you don't feel like hearing my sad story on a Saturday night." And just like that, compassion elbowed indigestion out of the way.

The "day drawing near" that the pastor of Hebrews refers to in 10:25 is the moment when Christ will return to judge the wicked and claim His bride. Remember how in the very first video session we established that we're living in the "latter" or "last" days—the time period between the first and second coming of Jesus? We're experiencing "the already but the not yet"—mankind has already witnessed the first coming of Jesus Christ. And if you've put your hope in His sacrificial death on the cross and subsequent resurrection, you are already reconciled to God. The debt of your sin has been completely paid for. However, we're not yet glorified. This spinning planet is not yet our home. On the day drawing near, Jesus will come a second time; He'll ride in on a white horse and escort believers to the New Jerusalem. And, oh, what a day of rejoicing that will be!

I said, "My name's Lisa and this is Jen, and we'd love to hear your story." And that was all it took to open the door to Jason's heart. His wife had been murdered in a fast-food robbery in the fall of 2011, and he was raising their three young children alone. The details of the last two years of his life were heartbreaking. He teared up while talking about how much he missed his wife and how much he wished she could be there to see their youngest daughter start kindergarten.

Jason's raw authenticity gave us the perfect opportunity to talk about God's tangible comfort during life's most painful seasons. How the Bible promises that He's close to the brokenhearted and near to us when we feel crushed (Psalm 34:18). Jason's face lit up and he began sharing enthusiastically about how God had been the core of their healing process from the very beginning. A smile spread across his face when he described their oldest son (who was nine at the time) walking into his bedroom the morning after his mama was killed and saying, "Daddy, I think we need to start going to church."

The last five minutes of our ride turned into a revival as we swapped stories about how loving and accessible God is. Instead of simply being a mode of transportation from a restaurant to our hotel, his cab became a rolling church service. It reminded me of how believers need to hang out together, to share the cool stuff Christ is doing in our lives, and galvanize each other by testifying how great our Redeemer really is. Genuine Christian community—a tribe of other like-minded friends who cheer us on not necessarily because we're good, but because God is good and we have Him in common—is such a gift. I think that kind of community is an absolute necessity for radical Christian living. If we don't want to get banged up and bloodied on the rocks of self-pity and discouragement, we need to both engage in a community of faith and encourage others in our community.

Let's not forget that our God is a Trinitarian God who exists in real relationship. God said, "Let us make man in *our image*, after *our likeness*" (Gen. 1:26; emphasis mine). God is an us! In other words, God the Father, God the Son, and God the Spirit rule and reign in perfect symbiotic unity (also known as "ontological equality," as mentioned in week 1): God the Father planned our redemption, Christ the Son accomplished our redemption, and the Holy Spirit affirms and applies our redemption. They are a divine symphony of righteousness, mercy, and grace.

Isolation is so not an issue in glory. Furthermore, since Jesus taught His disciples to pray, "Your kingdom come. Your will be done on earth as it is in heaven" (Matt. 6:10, HCSB), it's clear that God wants us to flourish in healthy community with each other here on this broken planet too. The word "encouraging" in Hebrews 10:25 comes from the Greek root word *parakaleō*, which means "to ask, beg, plead; to comfort, exhort, urge; to call, invite."[1]

Who have you pleaded with to move toward Jesus or urged to reengage in Christian fellowship recently?

Do you consider yourself more of a verbal encourager or more of an action-oriented encourager?

Describe a recent "encouraging encounter" in which you used either words or actions to affirm a friend.

Read Ecclesiastes 4:9-12. Which one or two Christ-following friends make up the strongest multi-cord community in your life this season?

What do you think is the key to your cohesiveness?

SCOOT YOUR CHAIR A LITTLE CLOSER TO JESUS

Once you get past the "tips" part of this passage and commit to flying down the hill of radical Christian living, a couple of moguls can throw you off course. The first one in Hebrews 10:26-31 covers the sticky eternal-security ground that we've already covered in the video segment on the problematic passages panel with Paige and Dale, so we're going to pass over it to the big bump at the end:

> Remember the earlier days when, after you had been enlightened, you endured a hard struggle with sufferings. Sometimes you were publicly exposed to taunts and afflictions, and at other times you were companions of those who were treated that way. For you sympathized with the prisoners and accepted with joy the confiscation of your possessions, knowing that you yourselves have a better and enduring possession. So don't throw away your confidence, which has a great reward. For you need endurance, so that after you have done God's will, you may receive what was promised.
>
> For yet in a very little while,
> the Coming One will come and not delay.
>
> But My righteous one will live by faith;
> and if he draws back,
> I have no pleasure in him.
>
> But we are not those who draw back and are destroyed,
> but those who have faith and obtain life.
>
> **HEBREWS 10:32-39 (HCSB)**

The motley crew of Jewish converts were in familiar territory—bruised and bloodied for the sake of the gospel. They have endured extreme abuse. They've been called names that would make a sailor blush, had their homes vandalized, their property stolen, been punched in the face, and subjected to Roman shakedowns that left them helplessly watching as their friends were hauled off to jail or lit on fire at one of Nero's wicked parties. And they did so joyfully (verse 34). But they've been bullied for about as long as they can stand it now. Their tails are drooping and their spirits are sagging. The passion that once fueled them to stand firm in the face of persecution has ebbed.

So their shepherd does what all great ski coaches do when their racers are intimidated by a tough course or tough competition: he revs them up by recalling their previous victories, reminding them that down-hilling bravery runs in their blood. Then he points to the glimmering trophy of abundant and eternal life on the other side of the finish line for those who don't give up. Finally, in Hebrews 10:37-38 he intentionally pokes his spiritual athletes' soft spot by quoting Habakkuk and bringing up the possibility that some of them might actually chicken out. Two life-changing questions hang in the air after his pre-race speech. Try them out yourself; they're still valid questions today:

Do you still think following Jesus is worth the cost?

Are you still convinced that His treasure is better than anything the world offers? Why or why not?

I think it's fitting that we end week 5 by ruminating on a similar challenge issued by another inspirational Christian "coach" named Thomas à Kempis, who penned these words several centuries ago:

> Jesus hath now many lovers of his heavenly kingdom, but few bearers of his cross. He hath many desirous of comfort, but few of tribulation. He findeth many companions of his table, but few of his abstinence. All desire to rejoice with him, few are willing to endure anything for him, or with him. Many follow Jesus unto the breaking of the bread, but few to the drinking of the cup of his passion. Many reverence his miracles, few follow the ignominy of his cross. Many love Jesus as long as adversities happen not. Many praise and bless him, so long as they receive any consolations from him. But if Jesus hide himself, and leave them but a little while, they fall either into complaining, or into too much dejection of mind. But they who love Jesus for the sake of Jesus, and not for some special comfort of their own, bless him in all tribulation and anguish of heart, as well as in the state of highest comfort. And although he should never be willing to give them comfort, they notwithstanding would ever praise him, and wish to be always giving thanks. O, how powerful is the pure love of Jesus, which is mixed with no self-interest, or self-love!

Dear God, may it be so. May we love Jesus for Jesus and not for any comfort of our own.

LIVE THE STORY OUT LOUD

1. *Read Acts 11–15 and consider the three biggest Barnabas-like encouragers God blessed you with during three seasons of your life.*

   During your childhood ...

   In your adolescence ...

   During adulthood ...

2. *Write your three significant encouragers a letter or card, thanking them for the way they spurred you on in your walk of faith. If your Barnabases are deceased, address the note to their spouse or one of their children, explaining how much they meant to you.*

3. *You may have already noticed that Hebrews 10:19-25 begins with an appeal (a tip!) to have faith, followed by an appeal to hope, and then concludes with an appeal to love. Use a concordance to find several verses for each appeal and then write your favorite verse regarding hope, faith, and love on individual index cards and read all three out loud to yourself every day this week (by the way, I've discovered that reciting verses when I run or hike is a great way to distract my mind from my aching hips and knees!).*

4. *Take a mental inventory of people in your family or circle of friends who need a little extra encouragement and choose one to spur on this week. Commit to pray for that precious image-bearer of God daily and fast for at least one meal on his/her behalf. Call or email him/her at some point to offer some tangible encouragement.*

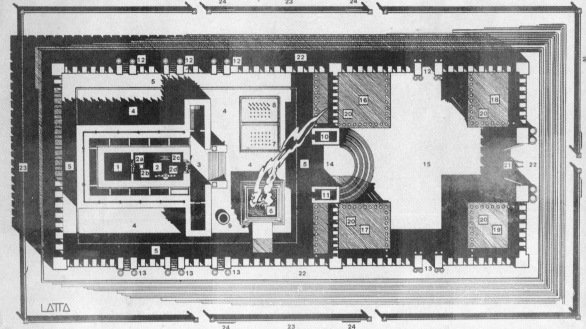

For enlarged image with legend, see p. 152

THE VEIL

The term "veil" is used in both the Old and the New Testaments in association with the tabernacle and temple. The tabernacle was God's dwelling place (Ex. 25:8) and originated during the Israelites' wilderness wanderings. The tabernacle continued to play a significant role in Hebrew society until King Solomon built the temple (begun in 966 B.C.).[1] The fixed structure of the temple replaced the mobile tabernacle. The tabernacle and the temple were similar—and yet quite different. Among the most striking similarities was the veil that separated the holy place from the holy of holies in each structure.

The veil symbolized the unapproachability of God, whose presence was represented by the ark of the covenant (vv. 21-22). The veil served as a barrier, forbidding humans to see, and thus defile, what lay behind it (26:33). Prior to establishing the tabernacle, God instructed Moses to "warn the people not to break through to see the Lord" (19:21, HCSB). Even the priests who ministered before the Lord were not allowed to "break through to come up to the Lord" (v. 24, HCSB). Only the high priest was permitted behind it once each year on the Day of Atonement.[2] The penalty for violating this standard was death (Lev. 16:2).

Because the tabernacle was a portable structure, the Israelites took it apart when they traveled in the desert and reassembled it each time they set up camp. The roof, walls, and doors were made of textiles, unlike the wood and stone used for these same structures later in the temple. Notably, however, the veil separating the holy place from the holy of holies was a fabric covering in both.

The term for the veil that separated the holy of holies from the holy place (v. 31) is *paroket* ("veil," "special curtain," or "curtain"). The holy of holies was the most protected area of the tabernacle.

A comparison of 2 Chronicles 3:14 with Exodus 26:31 reveals the veils outside the holy of holies in the tabernacle and temple were both made of yarn—colored blue, purple, and scarlet—and "finely spun linen." The colors used were associated with royalty and resulted from dye extracted from various Mediterranean shellfish and the *Coccus illcis* worm. People associated the fine linen with Egyptian royalty because the fabric was so finely woven and sometimes indistinguishable from silk.[3]

Woven into the fabric's design were cherubim. The New Testament mentions cherubim only in Hebrews 9:5, a passage referring to the holy of holies.[4]

The New Testament speaks of the veil in the first three Gospels and the Book of Hebrews. They reference, either directly or by implication, the veil at the entrance to the holy of holies. In Hebrews 6:19 the writer mentioned a hope "that enters the inner sanctuary behind the curtain" (HCSB). The hope that enters the inner sanctuary (God's presence) is none other than the eternal High Priest—Christ Himself. He is both the reason for and the reality of one's hope. Jesus entered God's presence as a forerunner "on our behalf" (v. 20). Consequently, believers too may now enter God's presence, making the veil no longer necessary. A secure hope results—one grounded in Christ's own sacrifice.

Hebrews 9:3 refers to the tabernacle's "second curtain" and explicitly mentions the holy of holies. The writer cited the tabernacle to make a distinction between it—a passing replica—and the enduring reality of Christ (see v. 24). As the perfect High Priest, Jesus offered a once-for-all sacrifice, unlike the recurring sacrifices offered annually on the Day of Atonement.

The writer climaxed the use of "veil" in Hebrews 10:20 when he indicated that the curtain symbolically signified Jesus' own flesh. Jesus is that "veil" that leads to God. Whereas only the high priest could enter the holy of holies once each year (9:7,25), through Jesus' death, one can now confidently enter God's presence at any time (10:19-20). Barclay put it like this: "It was when the flesh of Christ was rent upon the Cross that men really saw God."[5] No wonder the veil of the temple was torn in two (Matt. 27:51; Mark 15:38; and Luke 23:45)! Thus Hebrews declares Christ to be the "radiance of . . . [God's] glory, the exact expression of His nature" (1:3, HCSB). At last, God made Himself known in Jesus, no longer to be hidden by the veil!

Hallelujah!

Adapted from "The Veil" by Martha S. Bergen, Biblical Illustrator, fall 2006, 6–9. For further study, look for "Hebrews: The Nearness of King Jesus Biblical Illustrator Bundle" on lifeway.com/hebrews.

1. H. G. Stigers, "Temple, Jerusalem" in The Zondervan Pictorial Encyclopedia of the Bible (ZPEB), Merrill C. Tenney, gen. ed., vol. 5 (Grand Rapids: Zondervan Publishing House, 1976), 627.
2. The exception to this would be when the tabernacle was moved (Num. 4:5-6,17-20).
3. The NIV Study Bible, Kenneth Barker, gen. ed. (Grand Rapids: Zondervan Bible Publishers, 1985), 122–123.
4. Michael Martin, "Cherub, Cherubim" in Holman Bible Dictionary, Trent C. Butler, gen. ed. (Nashville: Holman Bible Publishers, 1991), 247.
5. William Barclay, The Letter to the Hebrews, The Daily Study Bible (Edinburgh: Saint Andrew Press, 1966), 134.

Our God not only _____ broken people, He can use _____ ,
_____ people.

The Hero of Hebrews 11 is _____ .

Samson was a _____.

Three vows of Nazirites:
1. They could not get close to or touch a _____ _____ (unclean).
2. They were not allowed to _____ their _____ .
3. They could not partake of the _____ of the _____ .

The Valley of Sorek means the valley of _____ .

History _____ itself.

It is not our _____ that Jesus is attracted to—it is our _____ .

Video sessions available for purchase
at www.lifeway.com/hebrews

Discussion Questions

1. *How does it encourage you that God can use the bumblers and stumblers in the faith and that we don't need to be perfect to serve Him?*

2. *How does the supremacy of faith (rather than law) fit the pastor's overall argument in the Book of Hebrews?*

3. *How does Jesus' not being attracted to our beauty but to our brokenness change your attitude and motivate your actions?*

_____

_____

_____

_____

_____

_____

_____

_____

_____

_____

_____

_____

WEEK 6

FROM ABSOLUTE RUIN TO GLORIOUS RESTORATION

Since this is the last week of our study and our last time to sit down together and talk, I'll dispense with the formalities. The Holy Spirit has prompted me to share a very private part of my heart. So grab a cup of coffee and a yummy carb-laden treat, and let's talk.

When I was five, my parents divorced (after eleven years of intense discord). One of my earliest memories involves Dad physically abusing Mom, and me squeezing in between them and begging him to stop hurting her. I don't have any memories of a loving glance or a kind word passing between them. Mostly I remember an uncomfortable lack of conversation occasionally punctuated by rage. Their marriage didn't begin with genuine affection that eventually waned—it was irreparably broken from the beginning.

The bottom line is that Mom didn't love Dad and only married him because her mama manipulated her into it. And the main reason Grandmom was so keen on their union is because Daddy was a Nazarene—the denomination she'd been brought up in—so marrying off her eldest daughter to him was her subversive way of one-upping her Baptist husband. I never knew my grandfather, but was told that on his deathbed he said the greatest regret of his life was allowing Mom to marry Dad. It still makes me sad to think that religion was the wedge that forced my parents apart before they'd had a chance to learn to be together.

I know some people think the phrase "It's not about religion; it's about having a relationship with Jesus" is cheesy, but I don't. I think it's too true to be trite.

Please believe me when I say my dad wasn't a total cad. He was young, foolish, and easily angered, but more than anything, Dad was ashamed. Shame is the monkey Satan most often tries to glue to my back too. His parents lost almost everything in the Depression and lived the second half of their lives in poverty. When Dad was a teen, they moved to West Palm Beach, Florida, to escape the humiliation of financial failure in Tennessee and to make a fresh start at a dairy farm. My dad got up every morning before dawn to help his dad milk a large herd of cows, then he went to school and rubbed shoulders with kids whose parents were millionaires, and then he walked back to a shabby rental house to milk all those cows again before bedtime.

To say he was determined to succeed is an understatement. But then his depravity got in the way, and he got a girl pregnant during his junior year, forcing him to drop out of high school to provide for his family. That marriage lasted less than a year and left Dad in an even deeper pit of shame. He was only seventeen years old, and he already had a failed marriage, a baby boy he rarely saw, and a sore back from his job shoveling pine mulch into boxcars bound for northern cities. He often dreamed of riding one of those boxcars out of Florida and away from what his life had become.

His dream came true one day when a man in their Nazarene congregation took notice of Dad's work ethic and willingness to own his mistakes. He committed to pay for Dad to go to college as long as he went to a Nazarene institution. So Dad ended up going to Trevecca Nazarene University in Nashville, Tennessee, and rooming with another Florida boy, Vernon Brown. Vernon had a beautiful little sister, Patti, whom Dad met when he went home with Vernon on spring break. He asked Mom to marry him after a brief courtship carried out through the U.S. Postal Service.

Mom said she knew she didn't love Dad and tearfully told him so at the beginning of their wedding rehearsal. She said, "I don't love you, Everett, and I can't marry you." Then she ran out of the sanctuary before rehearsing anything. Grandmom found her crying in a Sunday school room, but when Mom explained how she felt, Grandmom said it was just normal pre-wedding jitters and that it would embarrass the entire family if she backed out. Grandmom wasn't a total stinker either—she was funny and was mostly loving and kind—but sometimes her humanity got the best of her. So the next day my mom walked down the aisle, wearing a white dress and the heavy weight of regret.

My heart breaks to imagine how emotionally devastated Dad was when the pastor pronounced them husband and wife, knowing he didn't have a place in Mom's heart. I think that sense of rejection—the feeling that he wasn't "good enough"—is what drove Dad to flirt peevishly with other women on their honeymoon. He was trying to prove to Mom that other women did find him desirable. Of course, his playboy public personality caused Mom to withdraw from him even further in private. And when his flirtations turned into actual affairs, Mom medicated her pain with large doses of resentment. Ultimately, they had a very ugly divorce and bitter custody issues. I wouldn't say they hated each other, but from as far back as I can remember, they were like the opposite ends of a magnet—repelled by each other.

So it came as quite a shock to my sister and me when Mom—in the hospital, recovering from major surgery in spring 2012—woke up insisting that she see Dad. At first we thought she was super foggy from the morphine and was asking for Dad Angel (our stepdad, whom Mom married when Theresa was eleven and I was seven). Since Mom was in such a fragile state (she was diagnosed with stage IV cancer, which had metastasized to her bladder, colon, and appendix, and she had just come through a four-hour surgery to remove as much of the cancer as possible), we weren't sure whether we should tell her that Dad Angel had actually passed away the year before or placate her with hymns and sips of 7-Up until she fell asleep again. Eventually she got so agitated about seeing Dad that Theresa explained gently, "Mama, I'm so sorry, but Dad Angel can't come visit you because he's dead." To which Mom replied, "I'm talking about *your father*. I need to see Everett!"

We were speechless.

We were still relatively speechless the next morning when Dad walked down the hospital corridor, trailed by his dear friend and long-time Bible study leader, Lee. After hugging us, Dad said he needed to speak to Mom in private and left us standing outside her room. Twenty minutes later he stuck his head out and asked Lee to come in and pray for Mom and anoint her with oil. Theresa and I stood there, stunned like moles in the sunlight for a few more minutes before Dad and Lee reappeared. Our normally taciturn father hugged us again and said calmly, "I love both of you very much, and I think your mother might need some more 7-Up." Then he casually walked away as if he and Mom spending time alone together was the most normal thing in the world.

When Theresa and I filed mutely back into the room, Mom was smiling. She told us she was convinced she was dying before Dad prayed over her, but that immediately afterward, she felt the fear of death dissipate. The next day, Dad returned to Mom's hospital room to pray for her. And the next. And the next. And the next. Within a week, Mom was discharged, but they kept chatting on the phone every day about Jesus, the weather, and whatnot like old friends. Well, actually Mom chatted and Dad listened, because he never had nearly as many words as the women in his life.

Over the next ten months—from April 2012 until February 7, 2013—my sister and I witnessed the jaw-dropping miracle of the redemption of our parent's relationship. What had once been a horribly ugly and tangled mess became a beautiful tapestry of grace, kindness, and genuine friendship. When his health began declining that summer (Dad was diagnosed with cancer long before Mom, and despite two major surgeries, it had spread to his lungs and become inoperable), Mom began visiting him with chicken soup, fresh orange juice, and her own bottle of anointing oil. She invited him to her house for Thanksgiving. I sat at that dinner table, amazed that my daddy was sitting next to me in my mama's house, swapping stories with my precious little brother, John Price, whom he'd ignored disdainfully for 40 years because J. P. is Dad Angel's son, and you know how stubborn men can be about their "competitor's" offspring. Yet, there he was, loving on my baby brother, who desperately misses his daddy.

I'm weeping as I write this, still undone by the unexpected sweetness of it all.

The doctor soberly informed us that Dad probably wouldn't make it to Christmas, but as usual, Dad stubbornly refused to follow orders. I will always treasure the sight of him nervously hobbling into Aunt Darlene's house on Christmas morning, only to be engulfed affectionately by Mom's three sisters, their husbands, and Uncle Steve (Uncle Vernon died when I was in college), who all treated him like a heroic soldier returning home from war instead of like their big sister's cheating ex-husband who'd been estranged for decades. I had to leave the room several times that day so Dad wouldn't see me cry. It was a family reunion I will never, ever forget.

Daddy died six weeks later, just moments after Mama made her daily visit to feed him ice chips and read his favorite Bible passages to him. And a week after that, she was sitting beside my sister and me on the front row at Dad's funeral. Perhaps a few people found it strange that his ex-wife was sitting front and center, nodding in agreement while his pastor talked about how the second half of Dad's life was defined by his deep faith in Jesus Christ and his private generosity to the less fortunate. However, by then Mom's love for Dad seemed perfectly normal to me.

I've long believed our Savior can redeem and restore that which appears broken beyond repair. Now I know it down to the tips of my toes. Redemption and restoration are the themes of the final section of this life-changing sermon we've studied together.

I wish I could hear your story. I know it would be like mine, combining pain and the miracle of God working in spite of and even through that pain. But until we meet together at Mount Zion, where we'll have all time for all the sharing we want, let me ask you to write as if I were there with you.

Think of the low and high points of your journey and write about them below. You may journal a lot or just jot down some key words in response to these questions.

1. What has been your greatest source of pain and struggle along the way?

2. How have you seen God redeem some element of your life that once seemed broken beyond repair?

3. What most makes you know that our Savior can repair what seems broken beyond repair?

As you read Hebrews 12:18-24, look for contrasts between the experience of the Old Covenant with Moses and the New Covenant with Jesus. Highlight one and underline the other.

You have not come to a mountain that can be touched and that is burning with fire. You have not come to darkness, sadness, and storms. You have not come to the noise of a trumpet or to the sound of a voice like the one the people of Israel heard and begged not to hear another word. They did not want to hear the command: "If anything, even an animal, touches the mountain, it must be put to death with stones." What they saw was so terrible that Moses said, "I am shaking with fear." But you have come to Mount Zion, to the city of the living God, the heavenly Jerusalem. You have come to thousands of angels gathered together with joy. You have come to the meeting of God's firstborn children whose names are written in heaven. You have come to God, the judge of all people, and to the spirits of good people who have been made perfect. You have come to Jesus, the One who brought the new agreement from God to his people, and you have come to the sprinkled blood that has a better message than the blood of Abel.

HEBREWS 12:18-24 (NCV)

How does the contrast of Mount Sinai to Mount Zion cap off the argument the pastor has made all the way through Hebrews?

The conclusion of Hebrews is also the crescendo. It heralds the second coming of Jesus Christ, when the proverbial drum rolls and trumpets blare as every tribe of God's children gathers to celebrate and worship Him on Mount Zion. Jesus has proved superior to angels, to Moses, to the Levitical priesthood, and to the Old Covenant. Now to crown Jesus' superiority, the pastor takes a look back at Sinai and forward to the return of the King. When Jesus returns, however, God's people aren't terrified like they were in Exodus a few millennia before. Exodus 19 records the Israelite's arrival at Mount Sinai. The Lord told Moses to instruct the people:

> "'You have seen what I did to the Egyptians. You know how I carried you on eagles' wings and brought you to myself. Now if you will obey me and keep my covenant, you will be my own special treasure from among all the peoples on earth; for all the earth belongs

to me. And you will be my kingdom of priests, my holy nation.'
This is the message you must give to the people of Israel."

EXODUS 19:4-6 (NLT)

*So before we get to the scary stuff, what was God's encouragement to
the Israelites?*

Moses delivered the message to the people and took their response back to God. Note
how the Lord responded to the people.

Then the LORD said to Moses, "I will come to you in a thick
cloud, Moses, so the people themselves can hear me when
I speak with you. Then they will always trust you."

EXODUS 19:9 (NLT)

Why did the Lord say He would speak in the hearing of the people?

What attitude was God seeking to build in His people?
☐ *awe*
☐ *familiarity*
☐ *trust*
☐ *fear*

In a sense God's success at Sinai was the problem in Hebrews. God wanted His people
to trust Moses as a bridge to trusting Christ. But the people had come to trust Moses so
much that they were now reticent to trust the Messiah Moses foreshadowed and who
was so much greater than Moses.

*What similarity do you note between Exodus 19:9 and Matthew 3:16-
17 (NLT): "After his baptism, as Jesus came up out of the water, the
heavens were opened and he saw the Spirit of God descending like a
dove and settling on him. And a voice from heaven said, 'This is my
dearly loved Son, who brings me great joy.'"*

Why do you think God so closely linked Moses and Jesus by the voice heard by the people in both instances? (Note that God linked them in many other ways as well, i.e., both brought a sermon on the mountain, both delivered five major addresses—compare Exodus 20 to Matthew 5–7 or the Book of Deuteronomy to the Book of Matthew.)

Note how the New Living Translation describes Moses' purpose in Exodus 19:9-10.

Moses told the LORD what the people had said. Then the LORD told Moses, "Go down and prepare the people for my arrival."

EXODUS 19:9B-10A (NLT)

In what sense was Moses, a prophet, preparing Israel and the world for the arrival of Jesus?

After consecrating the people to get ready for the Lord's arrival, Moses' instruction continued:

Mark off a boundary all around the mountain. Warn the people, 'Be careful! Do not go up on the mountain or even touch its boundaries. Anyone who touches the mountain will certainly be put to death." ... On the morning of the third day, thunder roared and lightning flashed, and a dense cloud came down on the mountain. There was a long, loud blast from a ram's horn, and all the people trembled. Moses led them out from the camp to meet with God, and they stood at the foot of the mountain. All of Mount Sinai was covered with smoke because the LORD had descended on it in the form of fire. The smoke billowed into the sky like smoke from a brick kiln, and the whole mountain shook violently.

EXODUS 19:12,16-18 (NLT)

Contrast the fear of the Israelites with the attitude that motivated Jesus in Hebrews 12:2 (HCSB): "[K]eeping our eyes on Jesus, the source and perfecter of our faith, who for the joy that lay before Him endured a cross and despised the shame and has sat down at the right hand of God's throne."

Is shame difficult for you to overcome? Why?

Why do you think joy motivated Jesus so greatly?

In what sense is joy a greater motivator than fear or shame?

For consider Him who endured such hostility from sinners against Himself, so that you won't grow weary and lose heart. In struggling against sin, you have not yet resisted to the point of shedding your blood. And you have forgotten the exhortation that addresses you as sons: My son, do not take the Lord's discipline lightly or faint when you are reproved by Him, for the Lord disciplines the one He loves and punishes every son He receives.

HEBREWS 12:3-6 (HCSB)

Hebrews challenges us to include fear, confidence, discipline, and certainty of God's love in this relationship that empowers us to face difficult challenges as we journey toward Zion.

Beside each of these aspects of our relationship with God, write how that element motivates or impacts you.
1. fear

2. confidence

3. discipline

4. anticipation

5. freedom

At the beginning of Israel's history, God's people were afraid of being zapped into oblivion by Yahweh because of the inherent sinfulness of mankind. But now God's people can rejoice in knowing that when our Savior comes back to call us to our eternal home, there's going to be a P-A-R-T-Y! We're going to be racing each other to the top of Mount Zion because Jesus has satisfied God's wrath; therefore, Christ followers will encounter mercy at the throne of God.

Here at the end of the Book of Hebrews, reflect on the pastor's overall message, the conclusion, and how your life intersects with the pressured ancient Jewish believers.

1. They were pressured to abandon their faith in Christ. How are you pressured to abandon Christ today?

In what ways is your challenge less than what the Hebrews faced?

In what ways might your challenge be more difficult?

2. They faced stark choices between the results of openly claiming or rejecting Christ. What consequences do you face ...

if you remain faithful to Christ?

if you turn away from obedience to Christ?

if you seek to take some middle ground in your walk with Christ?

3. Their pastor issued challenge and comfort in their predicament. How do you respond to a call to difficult faithfulness? Would you rather be comforted or challenged? Why?

4. The call to faithfulness included a promise of eternal reward. Which do you regard more highly—present relief or eternal reward?

5. At the end of our journey, write your summary of the pastor's message to the Hebrews.

The heavy burden of the law has been supplanted by the glorious freedom of grace. That means we're going to be engulfed in unconditional affection even though, apart from Jesus, we deserve to be zapped. Plus, heaven's banqueting table is going to be way, way better than an all-you-can-eat buffet of chips and guacamole, cheese enchiladas, and molten chocolate cake covered in vanilla ice cream. Everything that once seemed irreparably broken will be redeemed and made whole in Christ. He is the King and He has decreed there will be no more dying, no more crying, no more separation, and no more shame in the New Jerusalem, the place where God's family will be perfectly restored forevermore.

We don't ever have to be afraid of where the gospel is taking us, because God's plan has always been for our redemption. And that is something to keep the wobbliest of saints moving toward Jesus, even on double-Spanx days!

CHASTENING

Why do Christians suffer? For their faith, the readers of Hebrews encountered insult, persecution, imprisonment, and loss of property (Heb. 10:32-34). Such hardships began to sap their confidence (Heb. 10:35). Most Christians will wonder sometime what lesson God is teaching them through suffering. People persevere better when they understand God's purpose in difficulties. Hebrews 12:6 describes suffering as the Lord's chastening. How is the Lord's chastening an affirmation of His love and our sonship? To answer the question, we must learn what chastening means. Next we must view God's purpose for chastening in light of His overall goal for us. Only then will we gain insight into the mystery of suffering in the Christian life.

The word "chasten" comes from the Greek verb *paideuo [pie deu o]* and has two general meanings: first, to bring up, train, or educate, and second, to chastise or punish. It refers to the use of corrective discipline in a child's life.[1] The noun form *paideia* captures both of these meanings to express the goal of Greek education, the formation of the human person.[2] Luke expressed this idea in Acts 7:22 when he said, "Moses was educated in all the wisdom of the Egyptians" (NIV).

In the Old Testament the Hebrew verbs *yasar* and *musar* combine both elements of teaching and training with punishment and correction.[3] God disciplined in the context of His covenant relationship with Israel to draw the nation to Himself with lovingkindness (Jer. 30:11; 31:3; compare Rom. 2:4). The portrait of a loving father illustrates God's relationship to His people (2 Sam. 7:14). *Yasar* and *musar* are not applied to the punishment of animals or to divine discipline of foreign nations. They only describe God's discipline of His people.[4] Moses said to the nation of Israel, "As a man disciplines his son, so the LORD your God disciplines you" (Deut. 8:5, NIV).

The comparison of God's discipline to the love of a father amazed the Jews. Rabbinic literature frequently quoted Deuteronomy 8:5 and Proverbs 3:12 during the New Testament era.[5]

The Greek translation of the Old Testament, the Septuagint, often translated *yasar* and *musar* as *paideuo*. The translators had the helpful covenant aspects of God's chastening in mind, rather than the less intimate idea of Greek education.[6]

God's love expressed in bringing up His children contrasted to typical attitudes toward children in the ancient world. In the first century, birth did not guarantee acceptance, the right to be raised and educated, or even the right to life. Parents in the Greco-Roman culture could legally kill their newborn child. They often did so, especially when the child was a girl or illegitimate.[7] In a letter dated 1 B.C. a husband told his wife, "If by chance you bear a child, if it is a boy, let it be, if it is a girl, cast it out."[8] Parents did not feel obligated to cherish children or to make them a priority. Children in the ancient world may have received an education, *paideia,* but not necessarily as an expression of their parents' love.

God, however, desires to turn the hearts of fathers to their children (Mal. 4:6). Paul instructed fathers to bring up their children "in the training [*paideia*] and instruction of the Lord" (Eph. 6:4, NIV). A father expresses his love through personal involvement in raising his children, even when he disciplines. In the same way chastening by God says you have a

Heavenly Father who loves you personally. The writer of Hebrews had God's love for His children in mind when he quoted Proverbs 3:12 in Hebrews 12:6 to explain why God chastens. "Chasten" perfectly captures God's fatherly love for us. Since we respected our human fathers when they disciplined us, we should yield to God's discipline even more (Heb. 12:7-9).

> "Chastening" paints a vivid picture of God personally committed to raising His children spiritually.

Some form of *paideuo* appears eight times in Hebrews 12:5-11. This makes it the most important New Testament passage for understanding God's purpose in chastening. More harsh words for punishment could have been chosen. The word *kolazo* emphasizes corrective discipline but not the overall idea of bringing up or maturing as a goal (Acts 4:21). *Timoreo* denotes the vindictive character of punishment and the sense of outraged justice in the one offended (Heb. 10:29).[9] *Dichotomeo* means to punish with utmost severity, or literally cut to pieces (Matt. 24:51).[10] *Ekdikeo* refers to punishment for the purpose of taking vengeance.[11] *Zemioo* implies punishment resulting in loss (1 Cor. 3:15). *Basanizo* means to punish by torture or torment (Matt. 8:29).[12] In ancient literature these words referred to both divine and to secular punishments for crimes. Criminals often were punished with beatings, fines, condemnation to mines or quarries, banishment to gladiator training school, and sometimes torture. Slaves could be punished in any way their owners desired. They were commonly subjected to beatings, brandings, and other kinds of mutilation.[13]

However, the writer of Hebrews chose none of the above to describe the mystery of suffering in the Christian life. Instead, "chastening" paints a vivid picture of God personally committed to raising His children spiritually. Love and devotion to this goal stand behind God's purpose for chastening in Hebrews 12.

So what should we make of suffering in the Christian life? Scripture calls it unpleasant and painful (Heb. 12:11). No one should ignore this reality. Nevertheless, we must not forget that hard times express God's love and acceptance at the deepest level. God chastens so we may share in His holiness (v. 10). He wants us to experience a harvest of righteousness and peace as He trains us by His chastening (v. 11). Ultimately, God strengthens us through chastening so He can use us to heal others (vv. 12-13; compare 2 Cor. 1:4). Such breathtaking goals make the chastening necessary to reach them worth enduring. Consider the benefits to us of what Jesus endured. "He was wounded for our transgressions, he was bruised for our iniquities: the chastisement of our peace was upon him; and with his stripes we are healed" (Isa. 53:5, KJV). Jesus endured the cross and opposition from sinful men for the joy set before Him and sat down at the right hand of God (Heb. 12:2-3a). His suffering brought us salvation. Therefore, we must not grow weary and lose heart when we are chastened by God (Heb. 12:3).

Adapted from "Chastening" by William A. Chambers, Biblical Illustrator, summer 1997, 41–43. For further study, look for "Hebrews: The Nearness of King Jesus Biblical Illustrator Bundle" on lifeway.com/hebrews.

1. Joseph H. Thayer, Greek-English Lexicon of the New Testament *(Nashville: Broadman Press, 1977), 473.*
2. Everett Ferguson, Backgrounds of Early Christianity *(Grand Rapids: William B. Eerdmans Publishing Co., 1987), 83.*
3. G. J. Botterweck and R. D. Branson, Theological Dictionary of the Old Testament, *vol. 6, ed. and trans. David E. Green (Grand Rapids: William B. Eerdmans Publishing Co., 1990), 127–34.*
4. W. L. Lane, "Discipline" in The International Standard Bible Encyclopedia *, vol. 1, ed. G. W. Bromiley (Grand Rapids: William B. Eerdmans Publishing Co., 1979), 948.*
5. Jim Alvin Sanders, Suffering As Divine Discipline in the Old Testament and Post-Biblical Judaism *(New York: Colgate Rochester Divinity School, 1955), 112.*
6. G. Bertram, Theological Dictionary of the New Testament, *vol. 5, ed. and trans. G. W. Bromiley (Grand Rapids: William B. Eerdmans Publishing Co., 1967), 608–12.*
7. Robert Garland, The Greek Way of Life: From Conception to Old Age *(Ithaca, NY: Cornell University Press, 1990), 84–85.*
8. C. K. Barrett, ed., The New Testament Background: Selected Documents *(San Francisco: Harper and Row, 1987), 40.*
9. Richard Trench, Synonyms of the New Testament, *ed. Robert G. Hoaber (Grand Rapids: William B. Eerdmans Publishing Co., 1963), 24.*
10. Walter Bauer, W. F. Arndt, F. W. Gingrich, and F. Danker, A Greek-English Lexicon of the New Testament and Other Early Christian Literature *(Chicago: University of Chicago Press, 1979), 200.*
11. Ibid., *238.*
12. Thayer, Greek-English Lexicon, *96.*
13. Lesley Adkins and Roy A. Adkins, Handbook to Life in Ancient Rome *(New York: Facts on File, Inc., 1994), 353.*

A CHARGE TO GO OUTSIDE YOUR CAMP

> So Jesus also suffered outside the gate in order to sanctify the people through his own blood. Therefore let us go to him outside the camp and bear the reproach he endured. For here we have no lasting city, but we seek the city that is to come. Through him then let us continually offer up a sacrifice of praise to God, that is, the fruit of lips that acknowledge his name. Do not neglect to do good and to share what you have, for such sacrifices are pleasing to God.
> **HEBREWS 13:12-16 (ESV)**

Discussion Questions:

1. *What are some specific ways you might take a leap of faith and move out of your comfort zone?*

2. *How does your perspective change when you think about the sacrifices and suffering Jesus went through for you?*

3. *What key points will you take away from your study of Hebrews?*

4. *How do you sense God is leading you to "live differently" as a result of studying Hebrews?*

_____

_____

_____

_____

_____

_____

_____

Video sessions available for purchase
at www.lifeway.com/hebrews

_____

_____

_____

_____

_____

_____

_____

For more information on Live Beyond, the faith-based, non-profit humanitarian organization Lisa volunteers with in Haiti, please visit *www.livebeyond.org*

Lisa and Missy

ENDNOTES

WEEK 1

1. Scotty Smith, "Spiritual Formation and Discipleship in a Postmodern Culture" (class lecture and syllabus notes, Covenant Theological Seminary, St. Louis, Missouri, January 16–April 24, 2006).

2. Tremper Longman III, *How to Read the Psalms* (Downer's Grove, IL: InterVarsity Press, 1988), 45.

3. Derek Kidner, *An Introduction and Commentary: Psalms 73-150* (Downer's Grove, IL: InterVarsity Press, 1973), 395.

4. "Hebrew Bible," Encyclopædia Britannica Online, accessed August 6, 2013, *http://www. britannica.com/EBchecked/topic/259039/Hebrew-Bible.*

WEEK 2

1. Jeff Benner, "Name of the Month—Eber," Biblical Hebrew E-Magazine, May 2004, accessed August 9, 2013, *http://www.ancient-hebrew.org/emagazine/003.html.*

2. *ESV Study Bible* (Wheaton, IL: Crossway Bibles, 2008), 2359.

3. Quotationsbook.com, accessed August 13, 2013, *http://quotationsbook.com/ quote/14093/#sthash.CNOL4FL1.dpbs.*

WEEK 3

1. This commentary is directly from the text of *The Voice,* "Exodus 32:7" (Nashville: Thomas Nelson, 2012), accessed September 17, 2013, *http://www.biblegateway.com/ passage/?search=ex%2032:7&version=VOICE.*

2. D.A. Carson, *For the Love of God, vol. 1* (Wheaton, IL: Crossway Books, 1998), 298.

3. Steve Rudd, "The Levitical Priesthood," accessed August 16, 2013, *http://www.bible.ca/*

archeology/archeology-exodus-route-sinai-levitical-priesthood-levi-gershomites-koha-thites-merarites-aaronic-zadok-asaph-heman-ethan-abiathar-eli-sadducees-annas-caiaphas-ananias.htm.

WEEK 4

1. *ESV Study Bible,* 2370.

WEEK 5

1. *Hebrew-Greek Key Word Study Bible* (Chattanooga, TN: AMG, 1996), 2101.

HEROD'S TEMPLE
(20 B.C. – 70 A.D.)

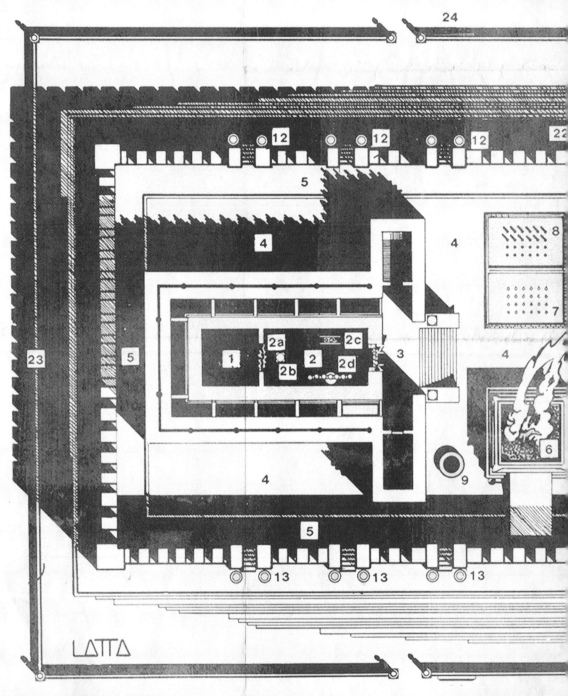

LATTA

152

1. HOLY OF HOLIES (where the Ark of the Covenant and the giant Cherubim were once enshrined)
2. HOLY PLACE
2a. VEIL (actually two giant tapestries hung before the entrance of the Holy of Holies to allow the High Priest entry between them without exposing the sacred shrine. It was this veil that was "wrent" upon the death of Jesus.)
2b. ALTAR OF INSENCE
2c. TABLE OF SHEW BREAD
2d. SEVEN-BRANCHED LAMPSTAND (Great Menorah)

3. TEMPLE PORCH
4. COURT OF PRIESTS
5. COURT OF ISRAEL (MEN)
6. ALTAR OF BURNT OFFERINGS
7. ANIMAL TETHERING AREA
8. SLAUGHTERING AND SKINNING AREA
9. LAVER
10. CHAMBER OF PHINEAS (storage of vestments)
11. CHAMBER OF THE BREAD MAKER
12. NORTH GATES OF THE INNER COURTS
13. SOUTH GATES OF THE INNER COURTS
14. EAST (NICANOR) GATE

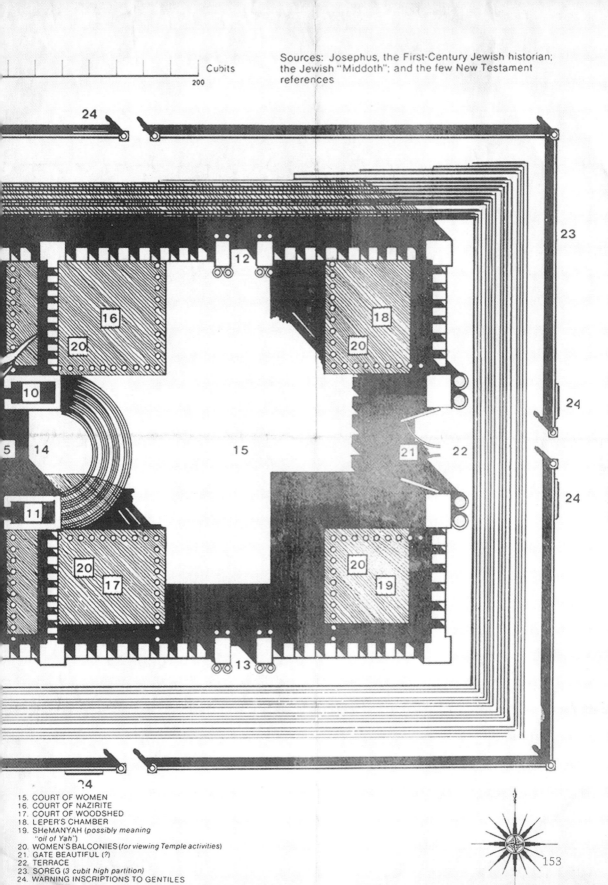

Cubits
200

Sources: Josephus, the First-Century Jewish historian; the Jewish "Middoth"; and the few New Testament references

24

23

12

16

18

20

20

10

24

5   14   15   21   22

24

11

20

17   20

19

13

15. COURT OF WOMEN
16. COURT OF NAZIRITE
17. COURT OF WOODSHED
18. LEPER'S CHAMBER
19. SHeMANYAH (possibly meaning "oil of Yah")
20. WOMEN'S BALCONIES (for viewing Temple activities)
21. GATE BEAUTIFUL (?)
22. TERRACE
23. SOREG (3 cubit high partition)
24. WARNING INSCRIPTIONS TO GENTILES

24

also by Lisa

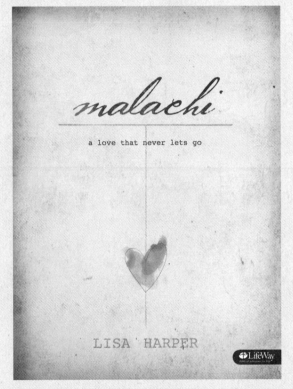

malachi

a love that never lets go

LISA HARPER

MALACHI:
A LOVE THAT NEVER LETS GO
8 sessions
God's mercy is so good. Even on our worst day, God won't leave us. And His love for us is not determined by our performance. Know God's unchanging love in a new way through the Book of Malachi with Lisa Harper's 8-session, video-driven Bible study. No matter how many times we mess up, God loves (and never leaves) His broken people.

Member Book 005474743 **$12.95**
Leader Kit   005474742 **$149.95**

LET'S BE FRIENDS!

VISIT OUR BLOG AT
lifeway.com/allaccess

Equipping You to go deeper into
God's Word

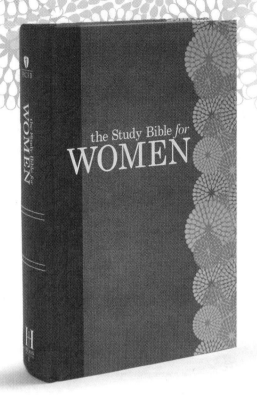

The Study Bible for Women is the most comprehensive study Bible ever prepared for women and by women. In this one-volume library of resources, authors trained in biblical studies and the original languages of Scripture provide an incomparable study experience to reveal the meaning, context, and applications of the text of Scripture.

DOROTHY KELLEY PATTERSON (General Editor) is professor of Theology in Women's Studies at Southwestern Baptist Theological Seminary in Fort Worth, Texas.

RHONDA HARRINGTON KELLEY (Managing Editor) is the president's wife and adjunct professor of Women's Ministry at New Orleans Baptist Theological Seminary in New Orleans, Louisiana.

Included in this premier study experience:

- The most extensive **study notes** published in a Bible for women
- An **introduction** to each book with key facts and themes, importance of the volume to women, and guidance for studying it
- **Content outlines** give a quick overview of each book

- "Threads" of specialized study woven throughout:
  - **Doctrines**: explanations of foundational beliefs
  - **Character Profiles**: background on women in Scripture
  - **Word Studies**: examination of Hebrews, Aramaic, and Greek words
  - **Hard Questions**: discerning answers to difficult passages
  - **Biblical Womanhood**: relevant essays
  - "Written on My Heart": **devotionals** on applications for life

A library of resources for women who want to understand God's Word and apply its truths to life.

Also Available:
Women's Evangelical Commentary
Old Testament

Women's Evangelical Commentary
New Testament